Where Birds Eat Horses

The Language of Evolution

Paul F Taylor

Just Six Days Publishing

Where Birds Eat Horses

Published by:
J6D Publications
4749 Spirit Lake Highway
Silverlake, WA 98645
USA

ISBN: 978-1515024958

Printed by Create Space

Comments

"The goal of the workbook is to help students and others think critically about the claims made for Darwinism. In short, Paul Taylor succeeds wonderfully in achieving this important goal. After discussing the basic common fallacies of thinking used by evolutionists in their writing, numerous examples from the evolutionary literature are presented that effectively illustrate these fallacies. First, some actual examples were given that were highlighted to give the student practice in applying the concepts reviewed in the first part of the book, then examples that students can do on their own, or in a group, were provided. Once these keys to critical thinking are pointed out, and the student is given some examples to practices, the student should be able to use these tools to critically evaluate literature intended to persuade readers of the validity of Darwinism."

Dr. Jerry Bergman, Speaker, Researcher and Author of many books, including "Slaughter of the Dissidents"

"Paul Taylor's WHERE BIRDS EAT HORSES engrosses the reader from the very first page. His brilliant explanation concerning 'fuzzy' words and 'magic' words are a real game changer in the analysis of the plethora of pseudoscientific declarations of evolution-speak with which we are continually pummeled. Paul has penned yet another stellar defense of the biblical account of creation. You must have this book!"

Carl Gallups, Pastor and Best-selling author of "Final Warning"

"Darwinian evolution is unscientific, unobservable, unbelievable, but understandable in a world that hates God. Paul Taylor is uniquely gifted with insight into this groundless and godless philosophy. May God use this book to equip millions."

Ray Comfort, Evangelist, Author and CEO/Founder of Living Waters Ministries

"Paul Taylor understands the importance of critical thinking! In a time when so many young people raised in the church are dropping by the wayside there is a great need for practical, straight forward teaching on applying our faith in a world that no longer believes in truth. Paul's book, 'Where Birds Eat Horses,' is one of those tools! The chapter on 'Fuzzy Word Analysis' alone is vitally important. Every parent and youth should be trained in 'HOW' to think, *not* 'WHAT' to think! My prayer is that the Lord will use 'Where Birds Eat Horses' to train many to do just that. To God be the glory."

Carl Kerby, international speaker, President and Founder of Reasons for Hope.

"Paul Taylor has done the creation community a service by providing a book that not only draws attention to a common problem with evolutionary literature, but has also taken it a step further in helping the layperson to spot these errors as well. In a society enamored with and too often intimidated by science, we frequently blindly accept everything in print when it comes from a scientific source. With wit and wisdom, Paul helps cut through the fog and exposes the "just so stories" that are too pervasive in education today. I highly recommend this book to anyone wishing to be better positioned to spot error and defend their faith."

Jay Seegert, Author and Managing Director of the Creation Education Center.

Acknowledgements

Thank you to Rick Spears for designing the cover, and to Jerry Bergman for offering editing suggestions for the text (however, any errors still existing in the text are my fault!). Special thanks to Mike Riddle for the suggestions for the book.

In particular, thank you to my wife, Geri, who made constant good suggestions along the way, and who is always full of good ideas. I am delighted that we minister together at our Creation Center.

Much prayer has been poured over this manuscript. So the most important thanks go to God, for His abundant grace and mercy.

Contents

Chapter 1

WHERE BIRDS EAT HORSES

Walking with Prehistoric Beasts was the BBC TV sequel to their popular CGI (Computer Generated Imagery) wildlife documentary of the supposed age of the dinosaurs. In *Beasts*, episode 1, we are introduced to a number of creatures, which are supposedly ancestors of today's birds and mammals.

Gastornis, from Walking with Prehistoric Beasts. License CCA 2.0

The first episode of *Beasts* stands out in my memory, as a drama of great power and pathos. Before we can describe my favorite, bloodthirsty scene, we need to be introduced to two important characters.

Early in the episode, we are introduced to *Gastornis*. This is a very large bird. Because of its immense size—it stood nearly six feet high, and its beak was a vicious-looking nine inches—we are told that it is carnivorous. Though not as tall as an ostrich, it would presumably have been larger and bulkier, and had a much larger head and beak. Interestingly, the program deliberately compared *Gastornis* to dinosaurs, stating "The dinosaurs might be long gone, but they left the world a vicious legacy".

Gastornis is named for Gaston Planté, who discovered the fossils in 1855. The "ornis" bit of the name is from the Greek, meaning

Propalaeotherium cartoon, Stanton Fink, CCA 3.0

forest floor, while staying alert for danger.

Then disaster strikes our mini-horses. They start grazing on wild grapes that have been fermenting in the sun. The voiceover (who happens to be the Shakespearian actor, Kenneth Branagh) informs us that the small quantity of alcohol present dulls the reactions of the *propalaeotheria*. They are drunk! If only the Salvation Army had been around in Eocene times, we could have had cute cat-size pet horselets in our homes even to this day!

The next thing we see is *Gastornis* spotting the little herd of adorable little horses. It starts to run, covering the ground fast, and snatches up a *propalaeotherium* in its beak. It shakes the little horse violently, until it is dead, then drops it, holds the corpse with its foot, and starts to tear off and eat bloodied pieces of horse flesh. Branagh's narration, which is sparing, reaches its height of inanity at this point, as we hear him intoning, in a deeply serious voice, with long pauses for emphasis "**this**

"bird". Planté discovered the fossil near Paris, but other specimens have been found in Belgium and England, and, most notably, at the Messel Pit, in Germany.

Another interesting character, entering stage right, is *Propalaeotherium*. According to *Walking with Beasts*, this creature is the ancestor of the horse. On screen, it is made to look horse-like, though it has four little hooflets on each foot, rather than proper hooves. It stands about 18 inches high. In the film, we watch a small herd of these alleged little horses, grazing along the (pause) is a world (pause) where birds eat horses!" If nothing else, Mr. Branagh provided me with a rather good title for this book!

Now let's stands back from the film for a moment. What is the viewer meant to experience? Is this education, teaching the viewer what sort of thing happened? Or is it a fictional account of supposed prehistoric beasts, like *Jurassic Park*?

The BBC has a mission statement. The founder of the BBC, John Reith, stated that the broadcaster's mission was "to inform, educate and entertain." This remains the official purpose of the BBC, in a statement which reads "To enrich people's lives with programs and services that inform, educate and entertain". *Walking with Prehistoric Beasts* could come under all three heads, but its placing in the "Nature" section of the BBC website would suggest that it is

one of their education programs. Although I am sure that they hope the program is entertaining, it does not give the impression of being a "story" in the style of *Jurassic Park*. So, it would follow that the BBC must consider the scene just described as a reconstruction of the sort of the thing that might have happened. While I would not accuse them of stating that this is an observational piece, when it has clearly been designed by animators using a script, there are a number of points that the BBC expects us to learn, namely that the small creatures are probably ancestors of the horse, and that the large bird is carnivorous, and is very likely to have fed off these little proto-horses. It is not churlish, therefore, for us to ask "What is their evidence for these educational points?"

The evidence, on which the show is based, is found in the Messel Pit in Germany. This remarkable site, which was granted a UNESCO World Heritage Site designation on December 9th 1995, is a quarry in Messel, a municipality in the district of Darmstadt-Dieburg, in the German state of Hesse. The Messel Pit was used

Messel Pit, Germany. Wikimedia Commons

for the mining of brown coal and oil shale from 1859 to 1974. In 1900, some fossils began to be discovered in the pit. However, in 1971, the intention to close the site led to plans to turn the site into a land-fill disposal site for garbage. It was at this point that scientific excavations began in earnest, and it was soon realized that the site was a goldmine for interesting fossils. A large number of interesting fossils have been found at Messel, including both the gastornis and the propalaeotherium. There is no argument from creationists like me about the importance of these fossils. What is more interesting, however, and of more concern, is the spin that has been placed on the finds, because of the juxtaposition of certain fossils.

The program clearly shows the propalaeotheria eating grapes. The narration suggests that the grapes have started to ferment, so the little propalaeotheria are slightly tipsy. What is the justification for this?

It is certainly true that fossil vines were found near the fossil propalaeotheria. However, that does not imply that the small creatures ate these grapes. Of course, they could have done so, given that they were probably herbivorous, but it is important to note that an elaborate fiction is being woven in the story, for reasons of evolutionary propaganda. The

propalaeotheria are being assumed to be "early horses", and therefore their evolutionary development requires evolutionists to consider them to be highly alert, and able to detect and flee from danger, in the same way that a modern horse would. The propalaeotheria are pictured in the program as similar to textbook drawings of what evolutionists claim is the "earliest" horse, known as the *eohippus* – which is Latin for "Dawn Horse". Eohippus is such a well-known name, that it is incorrectly assumed to be the scientific name for this creature. The scientific name is *hyracotherium*. This name was given to the fossil by the Victorian palaeontologist Sir Richard Owen. If that name sounds familiar, it is because Owen was noted for three things; 1. He invented the word *dinosaur* to describe the many extinct large reptiles that were being found in his day; 2. He directed that London's Natural History Museum built in South Kensington, London, England - more on this fact later; and 3. He was opposed to the new Theory of Evolution developed by his contemporary, Charles Darwin. Owen gave the name *hyracotherium* to the specimen, because he did not assume it was an early horse, but that it was a type of hyrax. The Smithsonian has a remarkable display, showing a fossil *eohippus* in the same display as a fossil tapir. Apart from the fact that the "modern" tapir is larger, the fossils look similar. It is very likely that the tapir is in the same *baramin* as the hyrax. All of this casts doubt on the classification of the Messel propalaeotherium as an *equid* (horse). But that would ruin a good story.

If the propalaeotherium had very sharp defensive reflexes, then, in order for the gastornis to catch and eat one, its attention would have to be distracted; hence the idea that the "horselets" were a little drunk, clearly impairing their judgment. Of course, there is nothing particularly wrong with such a scenario. After all, even today, a wildebeest will easily outrun a lion, yet lions are able to catch some of them, due to circumstances, such as distractions or that a victim wildebeest was slightly lame. The viewer, however, is being led to suppose that the imaginative scenario in the documentary was supported by the fossil evidence. This is not the case. The fossil evidence simply consists of a variety of animals and plants. The rest is a story woven around the evidence, using a great deal of imagination.

The last part of the puzzle is that gastornis was also found in the Messel pit. This bird is clearly a vicious, terrifying carnivore – the Eocene counterpart to the tyrannosaurus. Therefore, the juxtaposition of gastornis and propalaeotherium must mean that the

giant bird had, at some time, feasted on the supposed equid; hence the comment that I have used as the title of this book – "This is a world where birds eat horses".

Yet, in recent years, considerable doubt has been placed on the idea that gastornis was a carnivore.

In the United States, fossil remains have been found of a giant bird named *Diatryma*. Today, this giant bird is thought to be exactly the same as the European gastornis. The reason why both names still exist is that the North American fossil was originally put together slightly differently from the European fossil, making the two birds look different in posture. However, this discrepancy was sorted out in 2002 – about 130 years after its discovery. Wikipedia insists that gastornis is the correct scientific name for the birds on both continents. However, a recent article on the BBC's website referred to the bird as diatryma, although it did acknowledge that diatryma is thought to be the same as gastornis. What is also interesting about the BBC article is that it challenges the idea that diatryma/gastornis was a carnivore. Instead, the article suggests that the absence of talons and a hook on the beak of the bird "adds ammunition to the herbivory diet hypothesis". This article undermines the BBC's own documentary. So why would previous researchers have assumed that this large, admittedly scary-looking bird was a carnivore? The article gives what I think is a very good reason: "scary, fierce meat-eaters attract a lot more attention than gentle herbivores". So there was a desire among scientists, and documentary makers, to create a more sexy back-story than that of a gentle giant bird, eating nuts, berries and seeds. After all, if the fossil vines were found near the propalaeotheria, and the propalaeotheria were found near the gastornis, then the vines were near the gastornis, and it could have been the gastornis, rather than the propalaeotheria, which ate the grapes! The BBC's article concludes by quoting one of the researchers of the newer herbivorous story of the diatryma/gastornis: "The common belief that *Diatryma...* was likewise a carnivore is more a result of guilt by association than actual anatomical evidence". Guilt by association! The fossils are found together, and assumed to be linked in some way, so an elaborate story was developed to "explain" their juxtaposition. The truth, as is often the case, may be less interesting. Why would one assume that, if two fossils are found together, one has been preying on the other? The imaginative fiction created around these fossils does not constitute scientific theory development. It belongs in the creative writing class, rather than the palaeontology class. If the BBC's newer article is correct, then the entire premise of the scene from *Walking with Prehistoric Beasts* collapses.

Perhaps this issue could be overlooked if it were an isolated example. However, it is not. Here is another example from Episode 2 of Walking with Prehistoric Beasts.

The scene shows a large wolf-like creature called Andrewsarchus prowling along a beach. Kenneth Branagh's narration makes three things very clear very quickly.

1. Andrewsarchus would normally not be on the beach, but would be inland, hunting for large, grazing mammals.
2. Andrewsarchus is a very large, wolf-like carnivore – said to be the largest land-dwelling mammalian carnivore ever.

Andrewsarchus. Walking with Prehistoric Beasts. CCA 2.0

the mesonychids, which are supposed to be the evolutionary ancestors of the whale. Much of the same episode is devoted to the story of a pregnant female basilosaurus, which, despite its name, is not a dinosaur, but assumed to be an extinct carnivorous whale. A link is being inferred between the two, with the comment that andrewsarchus is

3. Andrewsarchus is not actually related to the wolf, because it has hooves. These hooves show that its closest modern relatives are not wolves, but sheep and goats. In other words, Branagh's narration tells us "it is a sheep in wolf's clothing".

Why are we being told these things? It is because the skull of andrewsarchus is similar in appearance to

Basilosaurus. CCA 3.0

being driven to the shore by changes in climate. It will be small step from watching it eat turtles, to watching it get into the water and eat fully marine life. The skull is also supposedly reminiscent of those of sheep and goats, and therefore the link between the *caprinae* subfamily (sheep, goats and antelope) and the *cetaceans* (whales and dolphins) is also implied, without being explicitly stated.

It is noteworthy that the hooves of the andrewsarchus are emphasized. Branagh's script reads:

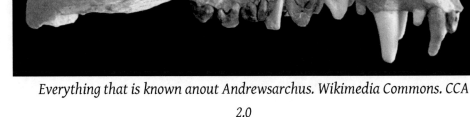

Everything that is known anout Andrewsarchus. Wikimedia Commons. CCA 2.0

Andrewsarchus, imaginative reconstruction. Wikimedia Commons, Public Domain

Bizarrely, he has hooves on his feet, instead of claws.

The fact that this is stated so emphatically would lead the viewer to suppose that the evidence for this claim is strong. However, Wikipedia has the honesty to admit that:

The appearance and behavioral patterns of Andrewsarchus are virtually unknown and have been topics of debate among paleontologists ever since it was first discovered. All that is known about Andrewsarchus comes chiefly from the single meter-long skull found in Late Eocene sediments in what is now Mongolia.

Do not miss the import of that quote. All that the paleontologists have is a "single meter-long skull". No legs, no trunk, no feet and definitely no hooves. It would appear that the development of the evolutionary link between caprinae and cetaceans is fictional, and not based on any hard evidence!

Documentaries of this sort tread a fine line between conjecture and false assertion. This is because they are made to mimic the popular wildlife documentary format. In wildlife documentaries, a semblance of reality is preserved. Even in these latter programs, scripting is in evidence, as hours of footage are edited to just a couple of minutes, so that they can fit with a script. But in CGI documentaries, the script is everything, which makes the narration at 18:54 in Episode 2 of Walking with Prehistoric Beasts so disingenuous. I need to set the scene for the description.

First, we see a herd of brontotheres. In the film, these creatures look a little like large rhinoceroses, with spade-like protrusions above their nostrils, where rhinos have their horns. These beasts are as big as modern elephants. The narrator tells us that they are related closely to both horses and rhinoceroses. This is interesting, because the classical horse evolution graphic shows the sizes of subsequent horse ancestors to be getting gradually larger. Yet here is an early relative - albeit supposedly in a branch line - which is not only larger than the hyracotheria or propalaeotheria from which modern horses supposedly evolved, but is actually considerably larger than any of those "modern" horses.

In this scene, a brontothere has given birth to a dead calf. An andrewsarchus is trying to get at the dead calf, to eat it, but the brontothere mother continues to attempt to defend its calf. While we are watching this scene, Branagh says:

It is impossible to know whether this mother realizes that her calf is dead.

Megacerops - a type of brontothere. Nobu Tamura, GNU 1.2

It is not impossible at all. The brontothere is not a real animal. It is the sophisticated product of a computer program, and the programmer has decided exactly how his creation will act under these circumstances. The narration, which implies that we are watching a real event, is deliberately deceptive, and implies a much greater knowledge of the behavior of these extinct creatures than can ever be possible.

Documentaries like *Walking with Prehistoric Beasts* purport to be giving a form of second-hand evidence for evolution. However, what we have seen is that the actual evidence is very slim. If the documentary only used the actual fossil evidence, then the program would be very short and very dull. So, what we learn from this process is that the evidence for evolution in documentaries of this sort consists not of hard science, but only of the use, or abuse, of language. The subtitle of this book is *The Language of Evolution*. Evolution is not a theory woven around substantive facts that is capable of making predictions. Rather it is a sophisticated fiction woven around real objects. When we start to understand this fact, we will see that challenging evolutionary ideas becomes very much more straightforward for many Christians. Not every Christian is scientifically knowledgeable. Indeed, it has

been my experience that scientific knowledge amongst the average churchgoer, as with the average person in general, in either America or Britain, is low. But knowledge of the use of language tends to be high amongst Christians in churches where bible study is common. So it is probably pleasing for such people to know that the real battleground on which evolution can be challenged is linguistic, rather than scientific, because the actual science in evolution is pretty near non-existent, but the use of evolutionary language is highly sophisticated. Evolutionists have become adept at using language, to sound scientifically literate. As we start to see what their linguistic tricks actually are, the edifice of the theory of evolution begins to tumble.

In these pages, I intend to uncover some of the linguistic tricks and manipulations used by the evolutionist, to provide fallacious support for his case. We will be looking at the use of devices, which I refer to as fuzzy words, and magic words - which are terms, whose use I first heard in talks given by fellow creation speaker, Mike Riddle.[1] I will show you the use of such terms in literature, in magazine and web articles, and in media - both fictional and supposed "factual" documentary. The use

---

[1] Mike Riddle, Creation Training Initiative, < www.creationtraining.org >

of such terms in museum displays, and other educational material, such as high school textbooks, will also be examined. And I will demonstrate a technique, which I have called Fuzzy Word Analysis, with which you will be able to assess the actual science content of an article or textbook chapter.

Before we close this chapter, I ought to say something about the use of evidence in support of or opposition to any stated argument. It is possible that my position on this subject will cause you to raise your eyebrows, because there are a number of traditional and popular creationist arguments, whose use I do not usually recommend. You will notice that my arguments begin from a position of assuming the authority of Scripture, and building my arguments on that basis. There is a clear biblical reason for this.

> *The fear of the LORD is the beginning of knowledge; but the foolish despise wisdom and instruction. (Proverbs 1:7)*

Without understanding that God is exactly who He says He is, and that His word in Scripture is inerrant, there is no foundation for logic or reason. An atheist will claim that absolute knowledge is not possible. It is the Bible's contention that absolute standards of logic, science and morality are not only possible, but exist.

This is the apologetic system known as *presuppositional apologetics*. I have written on this subject elsewhere, most notably in my forthcoming book, *Only Believe* - though my thoughts on the subject can be found in web articles and talks given elsewhere[1]. This is a difficult concept for many creationists to grasp, as they have often been used to presenting evidence to support a belief in the Bible. In brief, let me give two problems with simply presenting evidence. The first is that if you present evidence to prove your case, are you admitting that your case is only valid until someone presents evidence to the contrary? In fact, the biblical position has to be acknowledged by the Christian to be correct, even if a piece of evidence currently appears to contradict it. We must always ask on what basis the evidence presented is to be judged. Evidence alone can, in fact, be used to support entirely contradictory positions, based on a person's worldview. The second issue is the so-called Silver Bullet Problem. Suppose you find the Silver Bullet evidence that proves the Bible to be true. Which has the higher authority - the Bible or the Silver Bullet? The answer is that the independent evidence, by which you judge the Bible, must have the higher authority. The Bible

---

[1] For example, see my ebook, *Evidence vs Proof*, available from < www.justsixdays.com >

is only true, under these circumstances, because of the existence of the Silver Bullet. Yet the Bible claims to be the ultimate truth - the ultimate authority. Therefore, paradoxically, the existence of the Silver Bullet actually undermines the Bible's claim to complete authority. If the Bible really is God's word, then no such Silver Bullet can exist. And there are many logical reasons put forward in my writings, and in those of others, that show that there is no basis for logic or knowledge without the Bible being the supreme authority.[1]

[1] See, for example, the film *How to Answer the Fool*, featuring Sye Ten Bruggencate, or read *The Ultimate Proof of Creation* by Jason Lisle (Master Books)

Chapter 2

FUZZY WORDS

My friend and fellow creation speaker, Mike Riddle, has one overwhelming passion. He is concerned that many of the current crop of creation speakers are beginning to age. This particular author, for example, is 53 at the time of writing this book. We need new generations of creation speakers to carry the torch of biblical inerrancy forward, just a time when it seems that the majority of seminars and Bible colleges have compromised on Genesis. Therefore, Mike is concerned to educate the next generation of creation speakers, providing them with the tools they need to carry out their vocation. This is also my concern, and, therefore, I have followed closely some of the important issues that Mike teaches.

One of Mike's favorite terms is the concept of *fuzzy words.* Fuzzy words can be spotted all over the place in scientific literature and media - especially that of the popular kind. When I am referring, in this regard, to *popular* scientific literature, I am not implying that it is best-selling literature, or even that many people have

heard of it. I am referring to the use of the word popular to imply that it is written in an accessible style, so that many people could read it, if they came across it. In this regard, the magazines *New Scientist* and *Scientific American* are examples of popular scientific literature, even if you cannot always find the current issue in the magazine racks in Walmart. It does mean, however, that someone who picked up such a magazine ought to be able to follow most of what is written therein, without the need to have a PhD in research physics.

The term "fuzzy words" is probably best defined as follows. They are scientifically-sounding phrases, which give evolutionary information, but do so in a manner, which is vague or non-committal. In this way, information about supposed evolutionary processes is given, and yet not given at the same time, and, therefore, the evolutionist has covered himself, in order to minimize the risk of being accused of giving false information.

Like many such terms, it will be easier to see how fuzzy words are used, rather than simply define their use. By seeing lots of examples of the main phrases, you will eventually be able to spot their use a mile off.

Like most such linguistic constructions, the use of fuzzy words is not always wrong. There are some occasions where vagueness or a non-committal mode are necessary. I have even used some of the phrases, whose use I am about to criticize, in this very chapter! However, I am not going to draw attention to them. You can find them yourself. So it is not the existence or even the use of these fuzzy words, to which I object. The problem arises with the frequent, repetitive over-use of these constructions, so that no true information is being given, because no true information exists.

Different types of hadrosaur herded in the same area. Some had special bony head crests, possibly to identify members of their own species. (Emphasis mine)

What is the actual science behind this display description.? There are two things being asserted about hadrosaurs.

There is more than one type of hadrosaur

Some hadrosaurs had bony crests

It might be thought that there were a third fact being generated is that the bony crests were so that the hadrosaurs could identify other hadrosaurs. However, on closer inspection, you can see that is obviously not possible for the observer to

Possibly, Probably

The use of these two words is very common indeed. Many of the examples below, and in subsequent sections, were seen on exhibits at the Natural History Museum, South Kensington, London, England. For instance, here is a display about hadrosaurs.

New Scientist, Scientific American and Science Daily are all examples of popular-style science articles

Pachycephalosaurus head-butting. Wikimedia Commons, CCA 3.0

conjecture. Sometimes, these suppositions will be based on making analogies with existing living animals. Again, these musings can be justified, particularly if the reasons for the conjectures are given. However, I watched a party of school children filling in a worksheet at the hadrosaur exhibit, which included this question:

What purpose is served by the bony crests on the hadrosaur's head?

Perhaps the teenagers' teacher would have accepted "we have no observational evidence to support any suggestion as to the purpose of the bony crests", but I suspect that the answer he would actually accept would be "individual identification". It is in this manner, that the words *possibly* and *probably* get used. The reader thinks that they are being given information about the behavior of the dinosaurs, when actually they are simply being told a fictional story.

To illustrate this point, let us consider another exhibit at London's NHM.

Possibly, like today's rams and goats, Pachycephalosaurus engaged in head

know anything about the purpose of the bony crests. The museum writer has given us some *information* on the supposed evolution of the dinosaur, and its alleged behavior. However, it is not possible for an observer today to state how the dinosaur behaved, as we have no time machine in order to go back and make the observation. So, the idea that the bony crests were for individual identification is, at best, conjecture; a point admitted later in the same display:

With no living hadrosaurs to study, we can only guess at their herd behaviour...

It is perfectly reasonable to make conjectures about the behavior of these beasts, if such behavior is labeled as *butting contests to establish herd leadership.*

There is a sense in which this conjecture fits with my reservations above. The display has, after all, referenced the animals, which it is using as analogs - that is rams and goats. The text certainly exercises the imagination. The picture shown is from Wikipedia, which affords the opportunity to point out that Wikipedia's article actually disagrees with the head-butting theory, suggesting instead that the unpronounceable dinosaurs engaged in flank-butting.[1]

The same use of possibly and probably is found in the popular scientific literature. One of the most well-known source of popular science articles is the website Science Daily.[2] If you are itching for a new subject, perhaps it is time to consider a Science Daily article entitled "Did Dinosaurs Have Lice?". To save you a little effort on reading the article, let me tell you that the researchers concluded that the answer is "Yes". The lack of suitably sized baths for the application of insecticidal shampoo is yet another reason why

Allosaurus does not make a good pet. So, if you want to know the level of research involved in such a startling conclusion, here it is.

Given how widespread lice are on birds, in particular, and also to some extent on mammals, they probably existed on a wide variety of hosts in the past, possibly including dinosaurs.[3]

Sometimes I wonder if I could get a research grant to write such material. No experiments were necessary, to reach this conclusion. One is also reminded of the shortest poem in the English language, entitled "On the Antiquity of Fleas", reproduced in full below.

Adam 'ad 'em

May Have, Might Have…

The same Science Daily article quoted above uses a variety of fuzzy phrases. Related to the phrases in this sub-heading is also the little word *maybe*. For example, in the last sentence of the above article, it is reported that one of the featured scientists said "So maybe birds just inherited their lice from dinosaurs."[4] If

---

[1] The reference given is not for the Wikipedia page, but the reference that they in turn quote. Carpenter, Kenneth (1 December 1997). "Agonistic behavior in pachycephalosaurs (Ornithischia: Dinosauria): a new look at head-butting behavior" (pdf). Contributions to Geology 32 (1): 19–25

[2] < www.sciencedaily.com >

[3] University of Illinois at Urbana-Champaign. (2011, April 6). *Did dinosaurs have lice? Researchers say it's possible.* ScienceDaily. Retrieved March 19, 2015 from < www.sciencedaily.com/releases/2011/04/110405194055.htm >

[4] ibid

pressed, I am quite sure that the scientist would state that he was not giving information, merely making a conjecture. But it is often noticed that such conjectures have a great deal of influence, and today's "maybe" conjectures are likely to be tomorrow's "facts".

Now consider the following article, which was published in England's Daily Telegraph newspaper, and, at the time of writing, could still be found on its website. The article's title - surely an excuse for schoolboy humor - is "Dinosaurs passing wind may have caused climate change".[1]

The article's teaser line, after the title, reads: "Huge plant-eating dinosaurs *may have* produced enough greenhouse gas by breaking wind to alter the Earth's climate, *research suggests.*" (Emphasis added). Both the emphasized phrases convey doubt. Once again, the article's author would be able to state that he or she had not categorically stated that the Earth's climate was affected directly by methane produced from the digestive system of large dinosaurs, but the sentence puts the suggestion into people's minds for a reason.

Later in the article, we read: "Sauropods alone *may have been* responsible for an

atmospheric methane concentration of one to two parts per million (ppm), said the scientists." The article does, in fact, give a partial reason for this statement. In the previous sentence, it is stated that: "Modern ruminant animals, including cows, goats, and giraffes, together produce 45 to 90 million tonnes of methane". Now, it is safe to assume that this figure is correct. However, the article makes no attempt to justify whether or not 45 to 90 million tonnes of methane actually has a significant effect on global climate. There are many scientists - and not all of them Christians or creationists - who have serious doubts about the current prevailing global warming orthodoxy, which is exemplified in the statement about modern ruminants.

In London's Natural History museum, one dinosaur display states the following:

> *The large thumb on its hand may have been used for hooking branches, digging, or even for fighting.*[2]

The display of the reconstructed fossil skeleton of this creature (called *massospondylus*) is accompanied by an action-packed picture board, showing one of these dinosaurs hooking on to branches, and two more fighting. The picture clearly owes a great deal to guesswork and imagination, unlike the wording of the sober entry in *Encyclopedia Britannica*:

---

[1] *Dinosaurs passing wind may have caused climate change*, (2012, May 7), Daily Telegraph, < http://www.telegraph.co.uk/news/science/dinosaurs/9250032/Dinosaurs-passing-wind-may-have-caused-climate-change.html >, retrieved April 24th, 2015

[2] Text taken from exhibits in the Natural History Museum of London

London's Natural History Museum, Credit: Christine Mathews, CCA 2.0

The jaw was long and contained rows of thin, leaflike teeth suited for chopping up (but not grinding or crushing) plant tissues, although there is an indication of direct tooth-on-tooth occlusion.[1]

This seems to me like the kind of conjecture that is acceptable. No fanciful claims are being made, and the language speaks of "an indication", rather than trying to imply something which they

simply could not know. Even Britannica's wild cousin, Wikipedia, is creditably cautious in its claims:

> *Scientists speculate that Massospondylus could have used its large pollex (thumb) claw in combat, to strip plant material from trees, digging, or for grooming.*[2]

There is an honesty to the admission that this information is actually speculation. This contrasts with the use of image and description in the museum display, which lends an authenticity to supposed behavior, which is actually just speculation.

Conditional Tense

Sometimes, the conditional tense is used to make the meanings more fuzzy. This is not normally a legitimate use of the tense, if the condition is not given. When no explicit condition is given, it is often assumed that the conditional tense refers to a sort of "future in the past", as in the example below.

"By last Tuesday, he would have managed to achieve his goal."

As the tense's name suggests, however, it can be used to express what *would* happen, if some other condition were met - e.g. "She would have danced for joy, if she had

[1] dinosaur. 2015. Encyclopædia Britannica Online. Retrieved 24 April, 2015, from
< http://www.britannica.com/EBchecked/topic/163982/dinosaur/225953/Prosauropoda >

[2] Wikipedia article,
< http://en.wikipedia.org/wiki/Massospondylus >

achieved success in her exam."

Therefore, the conditional tense is usually characterized by the use of the words *would have*. Note how this tense is used in London's Natural History Museum display about a dinosaur called Tuojiangosaurus - a relative of stegosaurus.

Sauropods, Gerhard Boeggemann, CCA 2.5

> *The rows of tall plates running along its back, together with two pairs of sharp tail spikes, would have discouraged the hungriest meat-eater.*

Imagine a high school exam question; what is the purpose for the two pairs of sharp tail spikes on a tuojiangosaurus? Presumably, a teacher asking such a question would be looking for an answer saying something along the lines of:

"The tall plates were there for defense against carnivorous dinosaurs."

However, the display text does not actually make such a claim, although that claim is implied. Instead, there is an unwritten, hidden condition to the sentence.

> *The rows of tall plates running along its back, together with two pairs of sharp tail spikes, would have discouraged the*

> *hungriest meat-eater, if that is indeed what the tail spikes were for.*

Such a qualification would, however, destroy the evolutionary narrative, that requires fabricated information to be disseminated, in a manner which mitigates against it being interpreted as anything other than factual.

Two examples of this use of the conditional tense are quoted below, taken from the Telegraph articles mentioned earlier.

> *Like huge cows, the mighty sauropods would have generated enormous quantities of methane.[1]*

> *Global methane emissions from the animals would have amounted to around 472 million tonnes per year, the scientists calculated.*

---

[1] *Ob cit*

The first sentence should be translated as follows:

"The sauropods would have generated enormous quantities of methane, if we imagine them to be like huge cows."

However, it is more likely that it will be understood as:

"The sauropods generated enormous amounts of methane, because they were just like huge cows."

There is a subtle difference between these phrases. I suggest that article authors intend the latter meaning, but will rely on the former meaning for convenience, if they are challenged.

The second quote builds on the first, without referencing it. It appears in a much later part of the article, but cannot be understood without the first. Basically, it means this:

"Global methane emissions from the animals would have amounted to around 472 million tonnes per year, the scientists calculated, based on the idea that these sauropods were like huge cows." As stated above, none of these comments would be relevant, without an *a priori* commitment to modern concepts of Anthropogenic Climate Change.

The Unanswered Question

This can be a difficult concept to spot. Sometimes, questions are posed, which are rhetorical, in that no answer is required.

However, in the process of posing the question, a large amount of "information" is transmitted to the reader or viewer.

For example, consider London's Natural History Museum display about the allosaurus.

Remains of these large hunters are hardly ever found together. Did they live alone like leopards, carefully avoiding competitors?

Many children's dinosaur books show allosaurus with stripes, like a tiger, or spots like a leopard. A clear link is being drawn between allosaurus and large carnivorous, hunting mammals. However, notice how subtle the above sentence is. First, the allosaurus was described as a hunter. The fossil skeleton of the creature does not, actually, qualify us to say a great deal about the animal's behavior. Also, an inference is being drawn that, because fossil allosauruses are not often found together, that the animal must have hunted alone. This also does not apply. Finally, and most importantly for this section, notice the use of the unanswered question: "Did they live alone like leopards, carefully avoiding competitors?" Well? Did they? How can we possibly know? The fact that we do not know s illustrated by the use of a question, but the phrasing is disingenuous, as it is inside of this question that the inference that allosauruses behave like big cats is made.

The display continues:

Their size would make it difficult to chase victims for long periods. Did they use ambush tactics like the polar bear?

Allosaurus, drawing by Nobu Tamura, GNU license 1.2

First the allosaurs were like cats, now they are like polar bears! It is likely that you now have, in your mind, a picture of allosaurus, hunting its prey alone, yet ambushing its prey, where it knows the devastation caused will be at its greatest. But at no point has the author of these excerpts actually told you for definite that they know what happened. Yet it seems that there are many people who will wax lyrical about these "facts", which have never actually been stated, except as unanswered questions.

Now there is clearly a legitimate use for unanswered questions, and this use is in the realm of rhetoric. It would be perfectly acceptable for a display or textbook to use an unanswered question if the answer was obviously "yes" (or maybe a "no). An example of such a question would be "does the cat have sharp, retractable claws?" The information being provided by such an unanswered question is unambiguous, but

is not of the same type as "Did they use ambush tactics like the polar bear?" The answer to this question is clearly "who knows?" I do not have Doctor Who's Tardis to go back and find out. Again, it is not the use of conjecture, to which I object. It is the insinuation that the conjecture is offered as if fact.

Imagination

A step beyond the use of insinuation and innuendo is the unbridled use of imagination. It is important to emphasize that there is also a legitimate use of imagination. All scientists - whether evolutionist or creationist - will use imagination. For example, a picture book on dinosaurs might well show some of these creatures in a forest of gymnosperms - non-flowering plants. No one was able to take such a photograph. No one was preset

Imagination used in dinosaur reconstruction. Marcin Chady, CCA 2.0

Dinosaurs. It is worth quoting extensively from his article, because, although a hostile witness, a believer in evolution, he sees the danger behind the use of imagination in its support. Early in his article, Gee shows that actually there is a willingness on the part of the general public to be consciously misled by scientists, simply because the public wants actually to know something about the lives, loves and behavior of these giant reptiles.

People imagine that we can actually know anything for certain about the lives and times of animals that lived hundreds of millions of years ago; animals like nothing else around today; which lived in ecologies of which we know virtually nothing; and which are preserved - piecemeal and vanishingly rarely - as fossils.[1]

to photograph the dinosaurs among the trunks of giant ferns. Yet this work of imagination is legitimate, because it is based on the observation that dinosaur and gymnosperm fossils occur in the same rock strata. Of course, evolutionists and creationists give differing explanations for **why** these animals and plants are found together.

Often, however, the use of imagination is left to fill in details that otherwise would not be known (and in fact still is not known). Even evolutionary scientists have baulked at this in the past. Evolutionist Henry Gee was very scathing back in 1999 in a newspaper review about the BBC / Discovery Channel TV series, *Walking with*

[1] Gee, H. (1999), *Asking Questions, Telling Lies*, in **The Guardian** (Newspaper), Thursday 18 November 1999 (also available online < http://www.theguardian.com/science/1999/nov/18/dinosaurs >, retrieved May 9th 2015)

Every action and every background in a picture of a dinosaur is a work of imagination. Picture from Dollar Photo Club, royalties paid

dinosaurs that look so convincing in (for example) the BBC series *Walking With Dinosaurs* are, in the end, products largely of human imagination and artistic skill.[1]

The desire for knowledge about dinosaurs is understandable. The create imagination which animates these dinosaurs is legitimate. The problem arises when the imagination is passed off as if it were general knowledge. Gee goes on to comment:

> The palaeontologist Robert T Bakker imagined this animal [Triceratops] as a giant galloping rhino - yet Triceratops is only like a galloping rhino if you can allow a ten-tonne rhino that laid eggs.

> Lifelike restorations of dinosaurs are collages of varying degrees of supposition based on make-do-and-mend comparisons. This why the restorations of

Notice Gee's scathing comment about the comparison between triceratops and rhinoceros. Because both animals have horns, they are assumed to behave similarly. But, even when I was a child, thoroughly indoctrinated with evolutionary beliefs, I found these comparisons troubling. After all, a rhinoceros is a mammal, whereas a triceratops is not. Gee puts his finger on the essential difference, when he points out that triceratops was considerably bigger than a rhinoceros, and it also laid eggs - or so we assume! Actually, we do not even know this last fact! No one has yet discovered triceratops eggs; one would need to find fossilized eggs, containing the embryos of little triceratops, in order to be certain. So, even Gee's own criticism of *Walking with Dinosaurs* contains unproveable presupposition.

[1] *ibid*

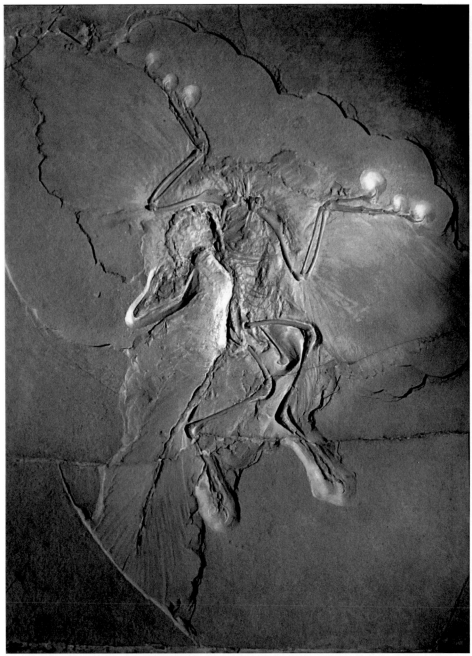

Archaeopteryx is described by Wikipedia as a feathered dinosaur. Photo by H. Raab, CCA 3.0

describes such restorations as "products largely of human imagination and artistic skill".

Neither Gee nor myself are claiming that there is anything inherently wrong with such use of imagination and artistry. For my part, I have exercised the use of imagination, in order to try to explain how I thought the pre-Flood world might have looked.[1] The point is simply being made that such imagination should be portrayed as such, with no implication that the imagination is fact.

Even as an evolutionist, Gee is rightly scathing about the preponderance of allegations about the supposed feathered dinosaurs.

Gee discusses the suppositional nature of even museum restorations, as being based on "make-do-and-mend comparisons." This is very significant, as we shall see when we look at museum and textbook descriptions of the behavior of dinosaurs. Gee correctly

To have found feathers in a non-flying dinosaur would have been reason enough for wonderment. Yet the first question journalists asked me was what, if not for

[1] Taylor, P.F. (2013), *Don't Miss the Boat*, (Green Forest, AR: Master Books), pp161-174

flight, these feathers would have been used for? The answer I always gave was that we could not possibly know.

Of course, feathers could have been used for all sorts of things, such as sexual display, or thermal insulation but we have no way of knowing this. We weren't there to watch. For all we know, dinosaurs could have used their feathers as offensive weapons, for tickling each other to death.[1]

Gee's sarcasm is particularly appealing to me at this point! Yet notice that even Gee has conceded the existence of feathered dinosaurs. While I cannot possibly rule them out (I have not seen one myself), the only real "evidence" for such feathering is the supposition - unproved and unproveable - that therapod dinosaurs were the evolutionary ancestors of today's birds. This unproveable assumption is manifested, for example, in such places as the Wikipedia article about Archaeopteryx. Wikipedia describes Archaeopteryx as "a genus of bird-like dinosaurs"[2]. This is in contrast to the parallel article in the more sober, professional Encyclopedia Britannica, which states that the creature is "generally accepted as a bird", simply observing that a number of paleontologists have called "for the reclassification of Archaeopteryx as a dinosaur."[3]

Gee is disturbed by the profoundly "unscientific" nature of *Walking with Dinosaurs*.

Everything in Walking With Dinosaurs is presented as fact, when what we actually have is varying degrees of uncertainty.

This is disturbing: the implied message is that we - the scientists, the experts, the authorities - have a licence to patronise you, the audience. If that is the implication, then it introduces into the BBC's science output an ethos that is profoundly unscientific.

Science progresses through institutionalised scepticism. We are taught never to accept the validity of any viewpoint simply because our superiors tell us that it is true. To present spectacular pictures of dinosaurs and tell charming stories about their mating habits is just fine. But to present it all as fact is authoritarian, patronising and, ultimately, unscientific.[4]

[1] *Ob cit*

[2] Wikipedia article, *Archaeopteryx*, < http://en.wikipedia.org/wiki/Archaeopteryx >, retrieved May 9th 2015

[3] Archaeopteryx. (2015). In Encyclopædia Britannica. Retrieved from < http://www.britannica.com/EBchecked/topic/32599/ Archaeopteryx >, retrieved May 9th 2015

"Jurassic Park" velociraptors, pictured at London's Waterloo Station. Photo by Ben Sutherlamd, CCA 2.0

If Gee were a preacher, I would be yelling "Amen!" The fact that Gee is an evolutionist is helpful to us in underlining the severity of the error. But if we assume that such "a license to patronise" exists only in BBC documentaries, we would be mistaken. For example, what do you make of the little speech by Dr. Alan Grant in *Jurassic Park*, made when a precocious and annoying little boy described Velociraptor as a "six-foot turkey".

A turkey, huh? OK, try to imagine yourself in the Cretaceous Period. You get your first look at this "six foot turkey" as you enter a clearing. He moves like a bird, lightly, bobbing his head. And you keep

still because you think that maybe his visual acuity is based on movement like T-Rex - he'll lose you if you don't move. But no, not Velociraptor. You stare at him, and he just stares right back. And that's when the attack comes. Not from the front, but from the side, from the other two raptors you didn't even know were there. Because Velociraptor's a pack hunter, you see, he uses coordinated attack patterns and he is out in force today. And he slashes at you with this... [he produces raptor claw from his pocket] A six-inch retractable claw, like a razor, on the the middle toe. He doesn't bother to bite your jugular like a lion, say... no no. He slashes at you here, or here... Or maybe across the belly, spilling your intestines. The point is, you are alive when they start to eat you. So you know, try to show a little respect.[1]

How much of that speech above is actual science? Of course, you might object that *Jurassic Park* is a fiction, and, of course, you

---

[4] *Ob cit*

[1] *Jurassic Park*, (1993), Michael Crichton (screenplay), Steven Spielberg (Director), Universal Pictures

would be right, but the character of Dr. Alan Grant was introduced as a scientist to inject "science fact" into the story. It turns out that his "factual" input is, in reality, no more factual than his equivalent in *The Da Vinci Code*, Sir Leigh Teabing.

Deinonychus / Tenontosaurus display at London's Natural History Museum. Photo by author

At least, Grant starts his speech by asking the boy to "imagine (himself) in the Cretaceous Period". So, at least there is an exercise of imagination. But then he supposes that the boy is familiar with the behavior of Tyrannosaurus. How could he be? Neither Grant, nor the annoying boy, have had access to a time machine to take them to see how T-Rex behaved. Assertions about velociraptor's behavior are, at best, conjecture; "And that's when the attack comes. Not from the front, but from the side, from the other two raptors you didn't even know were there. Because Velociraptor's a pack hunter, you see." How can Grant assume that velociraptor is a pack hunter? I am aware that Grant is a fictional character, but Crichton included this character, in order to provide a vehicle for the necessary science. But how much science is there in the statement "The point is, you are alive when they start to eat

you"? A comment designed to frighten an admittedly unpleasant child, would only be acceptable if it were true. But this statement has all the truth of the existence of the monster under the bed.

Of course, museum displays would not be guilty of the same level of imagination masquerading as fact, would they? See for yourself! London's Natural History Museum houses a display, featuring tenontosaurus and dienonychus. The interpretive text for the display contains four levels of imagination, each one building on the last.

Level 1

Fossil remains show Deinonychus to have been a fast, agile hunter easily able to overpower smaller dinosaurs with its ferocious claws and teeth.

Tenontosarus, Nobu Tamura, License GNU 1.2

There is an element of truth to the first clause. One can examine certain features of the fossil skeleton and determine that, perhaps, the creature was fast and agile. However, it might be better worded if it stated "Fossil remains *suggest* Deinonychus to have been a fast, agile hunter". The description of the claws and teeth as "ferocious" is more problematic. Creationists have frequently noted that the existence of sharp teeth does not necessarily mean that the teeth were from ferocious carnivores.[1]

Given the imaginary findings that deinonychus was ferocious, look at the second level of imagination, building on the first.

Level 2

---

[1] For instance, flying foxes (a large fruit bat) and giant pandas have sharp teeth, despite being herbivores. See Hodge, B and McIntosh, A., *How Did Defense/Attack Structures Come About?*, in Ham, K. (Ed. 2006), **The New Answers Book 1**, (Green Forest, AR: Master Books), pp259-270

The remains of several Deinonychus have been found near the body of a much larger herbivore, Tenontosaurus. Did they hunt it in a pack?

This level also contains an Unanswered Question - see the previous section. The first level assumes that deinonychus could easily attack small herbivores. But why would the fact that several deinonychus were found near the fossil of a tenontosaurus imply that the latter was hunted by a pack of the former? Did the hunters and prey all suddenly drop dead and get fossilized? Surely evolutionary paleontologists are not suggesting that these creatures all died in a worldwide catastrophe?

To summarize: level 1 imagination has led us to assume that deinonychus is a carnivore. Level 2 has led us to assume that it is a pack hunter. Level 3 builds on level 2.

Level 3

The brain of Deinonychus must have been well developed in the areas of sight and hearing, vital skills for pack hunters like today's lions.

Having decided that deinonychus is a pack hunter, this 3rd level has to compare it to the lion. So, the writer of the display sign has to give this dinosaur attributes usually associated with lions, such as well-developed sight and hearing. Please note that this level of imagination owes nothing to the fossils, but is a third level of story-telling, built on 2 previous levels. Yet there is a 4th level to come!

Level 4

Possibly Deinonychus packs hunted in the same way as African hunting dogs, exhausting their quarry with a long chase and then all attacking together.

The final stage suggests that the deinonychus pack acts like a pack of African hunting dogs. Therefore, they now take on some of the characteristics of those animals. Yet both lions and dogs are mammals. The comparison of deinonychus to lion or dog is no more logical than that of triceratops to rhinoceros, as noted

Fossil remains show Deinonychus to have been a fast, agile hunter easily able to overpower smaller dinosaurs with its ferocious claws and teeth.

*Text taken from exhibits in the Natural History Museum of London

above. These 4 layers of imagination, however, are captured in the museum's display, where a large artwork shows the exhausted and terrified tenontosaurus being jumped on by 4 deinonychus. The artist's impression displayed is not just a work of imagination; it is imagination on imagination on imagination on imagination! And these 4 levels are offered as science.

Summary and Conclusion

In this chapter, we have defined what we refer to as *fuzzy words*. We have seen that these are identifiable in museum displays, science articles, text books, and TV documentaries. We have identified a number of different types of fuzzy words, including the use of unanswered questions and imagination. All of the fuzzy word constructions are used to enable vagaries and doubtful ideas to be insinuated as if they were factual. They are not factual, however. We have simply seen that the actual "evidence" for evolution is contained only in the clever use of language, rather than in actual science.

Chapter 3

MAGIC WORDS

At the start of the previous chapter, I related that I got the concept of fuzzy words from my friend and fellow creation speaker Mike Riddle. After I had developed my system of marking up fuzzy words (detailed in a later chapter), I shared my thoughts with Mike, and he explained about another classification of evolutionary language - *magic words.*

Magic words are an interesting concept. They describe a phenomenon which is clearly impossible from all that we know about physical science, but that the evolutionist insists must have happened, if enough time is available.

Why would anyone believe something which is impossible? Why indeed! The concept puts one in mind of the conversation between the White Queen and Alice,l in Carroll's famous book.

> *"I'm just one hundred and one, five months and a day."*

> *"I can't believe that!" said Alice.*

> *"Can't you?" the Queen said in a pitying tone. "Try again: draw a long breath, and shut your eyes."*

> *Alice laughed. "There's no use trying," she said: "one can't believe impossible things."*

> *"I daresay you haven't had much practice," said the Queen. "When I was your age, I always did it for half-an-hour a day. Why, sometimes I've believed as many as six impossible things before breakfast."*[1]

There are a number of things that I find fascinating in this dialogue. As is frequently the case in Carroll's Alice books, it is the 7½-year-old little girl who seems to speak with maturity, and the adults who lack maturity, even though these adults are convinced that their foolishness is wisdom. Therefore, the Queen takes on the role of patronizing tutor, speaking to Alice "in a

---

[1] Carroll, Lewis (1871), *Through the Looking Glass, and what Alice Found there*, Millennium Fulcrum Edition 1.7 (Kindle), location 513. If you have a different edition, the quote is found in Chapter 5.

pitying tone". She then encourages Alice to "try again" to believe something that is impossible, and implies that the belief in impossible things is something that gets easier with practice, rather like playing the piano. Indeed, she recommends that Alice should practice believing impossible things "for half-an-hour a day".

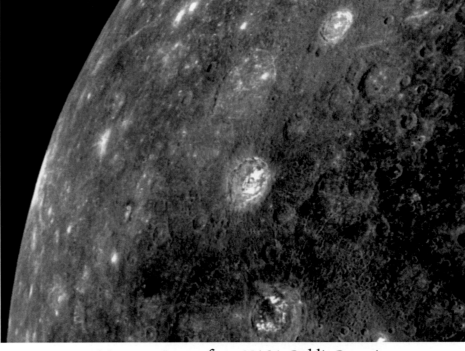

Mercury. Image from NASA, Public Domain

Can we really get better at believing the impossible? That would appear to be the case.

When I was a schoolteacher, I taught in the sort of schools that in the US would be called *public schools*, but in Britain are called *Comprehensive Schools*. I arrived at one school in South Wales. Most schools in England and Wales used to separate the teaching of Science into three constituent areas of study - Chemistry, Physics and Biology. For historical reasons, the Chemistry and Physics teaching laboratories at this school were in the same part of the campus, but the Biology labs were at the opposite end of the building. The Head of Science was also Head of Chemistry, so I asked him over coffee, during mid-morning break, why the labs were arranged so.

"It's simple", he replied. "Real science is done here in Chemistry and in Physics. Over in Biology, they just teach fairy stories about things that never happen". This comment came from a man who was an atheist member of the British Communist Party! Empirically, what he had to say made sense. In their Chemistry lessons, students learned about the impossibility of reactions happening against the flow of free energy, yet such reactions must have occurred for evolutionary progress to have been achieved. This was an example of something impossible before breakfast, as long as the breakfast takes a million years!

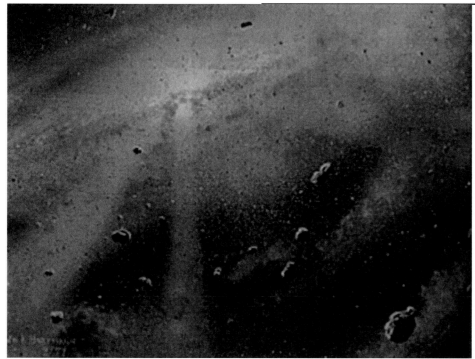

Formation of Solar System: Image by NASA, Public Domain

Take heed that no one deceives you

I have two main talks on Astronomy. One of these I give for teenage and adult audiences. The other, which I call "Counting Stars", I give to younger children. I start the talk by reminding the children of some words of Jesus.

"Take heed that no one deceives you." (Matthew 24:4)

Now, I am well aware of the context of this verse, and I am well aware of the danger of quoting a verse out of context. Jesus is warning that people should take care not be deceived about His return. But it is not unfair to use this verse in other contexts. Jesus does not want us to be deceived period. I can apply this particular verse to other situations. So I warn the children that some things that I say will not be correct, and that they are to spot which things they are, and tell me. And just in case they don't spot them, I promise them that I will tell them what my "lies" were before I finish the talk.

Next, I tell them that I am going to show them six photographs. We have some fun with these. Here is the first photograph. I ask them what it is, and most of them reply that it is the Moon. It isn't. It is the planet Mercury. Them I show them a crescent. They tell me that it is the Moon - but they are now a little more uncertain. It is in fact Venus. Thirdly, I show them an actual photo of the Moon, but, by now, they are too worried to say it is the Moon! So I reassure them that it really is the Moon. They relax when they see a picture of the Sun. Then I show them Earth (from the Moon - taken by an Apollo mission). Finally, I tell them that I am showing them a photo of all the planets forming out of dust around the Sun. Then I tell them that one of the photos is not genuine, and ask if they can tell me which one; and I show them the photos again.

There is usually a child who recognizes the odd one out. It is the "photo" of the planet formation. I explain that no one was there to take a photo when the planets formed, and, in any case, I don't believe that the planets formed that way, because the only eye-witness we have - God - tells us exactly how He made them in Genesis 1.

In a brief aside to parents, I try to point out how easy it is for children to be bemused and confused by pictures and by statements from "authority" figures like me. They need to know that children do not learn the biblical truth merely by being shielded from what the world says about science. Instead, at age-appropriate levels, they need to learn how to spot the errors coming from "authority" figures, and learn to defend their own faith.

It is easy for children to be bemused or confused by the concept of millions of years - sometimes referred to as *deep time*. Actually, it is very easy for adults also to be confused by such a concept. Time is such a very elastic concept for us, that its stretching off into near infinity past does not seem to be too difficult to accept, yet is horrendously difficult actually to grasp with our minds. But then anything that is ancient is difficult to grasp.

As this chapter involves the "magic" properties that seem to be assigned to deep time, I think that I need to walk down a bunny trail and explain to you why I do not like to use the term *Young Earth Creationist*.

Not a Young Earth Creationist

I am not keen on the term *young earth creationist* to describe my position. Please do not get too upset by this. If you call me a young earth creationist to my face, I am not going to punch your lights out! I would be too ~~scared~~ polite to do this anyway! It isn't the most important point to make, but there is a well-founded reason for my objection none the less. It is partly because of my commitment to *presuppositional apologetics*[1] This, in turn, stems from my commitment to the Bible.

I am sometimes asked how I calculate the age of the earth. I take people to the Bible, and show them how to add up the various ages and numbers. But some people are not satisfied by this - including many who refer to themselves as *young earth creationists*. This latter group want me to show them a scientific methodology or calculation which yields an answer for the age of the earth of 10,000 years or less. I can certainly find such figures. For example, I could point to the fact that comets in the solar system could not have lasted longer than 10,000 years. But this is not a methodology

---

[1] I will be dealing with the concept of *presuppositional apologetics* in another book that I am currently writing, provisionally titled *Only Believe*, which I hope to publish early in 2016.

to give an age for the earth for two reasons. Firstly, there are plenty of people who will disagree with me, and suggest that comets must have been around longer than this. The way that I answer these people is to show that their presuppositions are wrong, but, if I have to tackle their presuppositions, then it would have been easier to have done so in the first place. Otherwise, we are simply trading one human opinion for another. Secondly, yet this is a related point, I will also use a myriad of other "timing methodologies" that give ages for the earth or the universe of a million years or so. My object in so doing is not to suggest that I believe the Earth is actually a million years old. I merely use such a timescale to prove the impossibility of believing the Earth is **billions** of years old.

It is not too complicated to challenge the presuppositions of timescale calculations that yield ages of millions of years. The most well-known class of such calculations would be the various radiometric dating methods. I have given a detailed analysis of these in another book.[1]

Like me, Ken Ham has often stated that he is not keen on the term *young earth creationist*. His reasoning is the same as mine; indeed, it was when I read his

reasoning that I became convinced of my position. He states that it is not the age of the earth that is the real issue. The real issue is the authority of Scripture.[2] So this brings me to the heart of my objection.

Why do I believe the Earth is less than 10,000 years old? 10,000 years is supposed to be the "young earth" position. My answer to this is that I don't believe the earth is under 10,000 years old. I need more accuracy. I believe the earth is just over 6,000 years old. Am I nit-picking? I believe not. You see the "10,000 years and under" people believe because of scientific calculations. I believe just over 6,000 years because of the calculation I do from the Bible. This calculation is possible, because of my commitment to the authority of scripture. My presupposition is to the authority of Scripture.

One objection by so-called "old earth evangelicals" to the "young earth" position is that God is described as "the Ancient of Days". Their argument is that 6,000 years is not ancient. Says who? The argument immediately betrays that their presupposition - their starting point - is

---

[1] *Radiometric Dating and the Flood* in: Taylor, P.F. (2013), *Don't Miss the Boat*, (Green Forest, AR: Master Books), pp137-146

[2] Ken Ham has made this point in numerous articles and talks - too numerous to reference! I will reference just one. Ham, K. (2014), *What dos Bill Nye really think of me, and Christians in general?*, < https://answersingenesis.org/blogs/ken-ham/2014/02/17/what-does-bill-nye-really-think-of-me-and-christians-in-general/ >, retrieved June 6th 2015

unbiblical. How old is 6,000 years? Six thousand years is very, very old.

If you came with me to South Wales, where I once used to live, I could show you an "ancient monument", which is a neolithic burial stone, in the middle of a farm field. It is said to be about 4,000 years old. It is truly ancient. Wheen one stands and looks at it, one is filled with a sense of the "ancientness" of the site. Correct me if I am wrong, but isn't 6,000 years more than 4,000 years?

You see, I am not a *young earth creationist*. I do not believe the earth is young. I believe that the earth is very, very old. It is ancient. It is as old as 6,000 years!

If I am prepared to accept the moniker of *young earth creationist*, then I have accepted that I should measure my timescale relative to that of the evolutionists and deep time advocates. But the deep time concept of millions of years is not the standard against which I should compare different views. I should compare all views against the authority of Scripture. I refuse the term *young earth creationist*, precisely because 6,000 years is only young in comparison to unbiblical concepts of deep time. Compared to the biblical timescale, or our current experience, 6,000 years is not young. It is very, very old. So, instead of the term *young earth creationist*, I prefer the term *biblical creationist*.

The Magic of Millions

Look at a molecule of water.

There is a popular non-scientific misconception about water. Most people are aware that the chemical formula of a water molecule is H_2O. Most people are also aware that H is the symbol for a hydrogen atom and O for an oxygen atom. Therefore, a water molecule is comprised of two hydrogen and one oxygen atoms. So, there is a popular question, which you will find in many places on the Internet, which goes like this:

If oxygen is needed for fires to burn and hydrogen is a highly explosive gas, why does water not explode when exposed to fire?

The key error in the question is the assumption that water simply *contains* hydrogen and oxygen. Elemental hydrogen is indeed explosive, in the presence of an oxidizing agent, the most common of which is oxygen. When hydrogen reacts with oxygen, the atoms combine to form covalent bonds, which join them together in a new molecule, which is at a lower state of energy. A good analogy is to suppose that the atomic bonds in elemental hydrogen and oxygen are like highly taught, stretched elastic bands. During the reaction between hydrogen and oxygen,

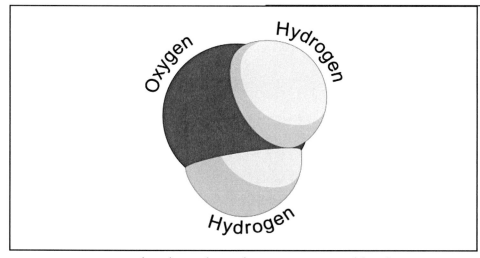

Water molecule: Wikimedia Commons, Public domain

In sheer chemical terms, therefore, it does not make sense to divide hydrogen and oxygen from water, and then recombine them to produce energy.

When I tried to explain this to one class, during my days as a high school science teacher[2], one child, who I shall call Jim (because I can't remember his name!) suggested that, if we left the water long enough, maybe it would just separate by itself.. I tried to draw energy diagrams to show that this would not be possible, but the boy was unconvinced.

"Surely, given enough time, anything can happen?", Jim surmised.

So John joined in.

"If it's impossible now, it will always be impossible."

Which position do you take? Do you believe that, given enough time, anything can happen, or do you believe that if it's

these taught bonds are severed, and the resulting molecules are stable, but at a lower energy level. Water cannot, therefore, simply be separated into its component elements, in the way one might sort dimes from quarters. To reconstitute the elements, one would need to do something to reintroduce the energy that had been lost. This energy could be supplied by introducing electricity, but this is itself a form of energy, so you are introducing energy, in order to get more energy. The Second Law of Thermodynamics tells us that the amount of electrical energy required to separate the hydrogen from the oxygen in water is more than the energy one would get back by recombining the elements.[1]

[1] Just as a bunny trail - this difficulty does not mean that this process has no use. If there is a cheap form of energy, such as hydro-electric power, or solar power, then it might be worth splitting the hydrogen and

oxygen by this method, as a way of "storing" the original electrical energy. The 2nd Law still implies that energy will be lost, but this might be economically worthwhile, if the cost of the original electricity is very low.

[2] I taught science for 18 years in England and Wales in state comprehensive schools - the sort of schools that in the US would be referred to as public schools.

impossible now, it will always be impossible?

Clearly, in the absence of any outside interference or input, John is the one who has made the scientific case. Yet, it seems all too common for evolutionary "scientists" to adopt Jim's theory. This is what we call the "Magic Word Hypothesis". Anything can happen, given enough time. The Queen might believe six impossible things before breakfast, but, if breakfast were long enough, perhaps these six impossible things might be possible after all.

A Case Study: The Origin of Life in Prentice Hall

One well-known High School Biology, Prentice Hall Biology,[1] will be useful to look at to see what it says about the origin of life.

Geologic evidence shows that Earth was not "born" in a single event. Instead, pieces of cosmic debris were probably attracted to one another over the course of about 100 million years. While the planet was young, it was struck by one or

more objects, possibly as large as the planet Mars. This collision produced enough heat to melt the entire globe.[2]

Before I pick up on the magic words, I ought to flag up some terms that we will use in the next chapter. The first sentence tells us what is "shown" by "geologic evidence". It is quite important to be pedantic at this point. Evidence actually shows us nothing, because evidence is something that we must examine. This evidence is interpreted, according to our worldview. Therefore, it is disingenuous for the authors to expect students to accept their word for this pseudo-history, simply by appealing to evidence. The appeal to evidence is much weaker than most people suppose. However, we will leave the analysis of this type of linguistic trick to the next chapter. Instead, let's concentrate on the sentence repeated below.

Pieces of cosmic debris were probably attracted to one another over the course of about 100 million years.

If you were concentrating on the last chapter, you will notice the use of the fuzzy word "probably". The reason for the use of "probably" in this sentence is because it is not immediately obvious that pieces of cosmic debris would be attracted to each other. They want you to assume that this

---

[1] Miller, K. And Levine, J. (2002), *Biology*, (Upper Saddle River, NJ: Pearson Education Inc), 2002 edition. I must emphasize that I am using the 2002 edition. In fairness, I must point out that there have been a number of revisions of this book. However, I am not aware that the text quoted in this chapter has been substantially altered.

[2] *Ibid*, p423

occurs by gravity, and that this attraction between such pieces causes lumps to stick together, becoming bigger lumps, until eventually planet-sized lumps accrete. But there is no reason to suppose that this would ever happen. For example, the asteroids are considered to be leftovers from the formation of the Solar System, which evolutionary cosmologists claim occurred 4.6 billion years ago. (Previously, they had once been thought to be the remains of a planet that was destroyed). In all that time, these small objects have not accreted into a large, planet size object, even though they are in reasonably close proximity, and mostly occupying nearly the same orbit. The existence of the dwarf planet Ceres, which is nearly spherical, among the asteroids is inconvenient for evolutionists, as it prevents their stating that spherical development is impossible among such objects. Moreover, there is no apparent evidence that Ceres was formed from accretion of smaller asteroids. So, there is ample material available in the Solar System today for such mutual attraction of cosmic debris to take place, yet it is not doing so. There were those who used to believe the hypothesis that the asteroids had formed from an exploded planet. While this hypothesis is not generally accepted today, its acceptance for so long is natural, considering that

separated objects do not naturally tend to stick together, particularly in the presence of other objects in the Solar System which have much more significant gravitational fields. In short, this sentence is an example of the use of deep time magic words. The mutual attraction of cosmic debris is not observed to happen, yet it is assumed to take place, if 100 million years are allowed for the process.

You might also have noticed that the accretion of lots of small objects sticking together in a planet-sized lump would not have the properties of today's Earth, which has concentric spheres of different materials, including a molten core. Let's repeat the last sentence above, together with the section which follows.

While the planet was young, it was struck by one or more objects, possibly as large as the planet Mars. This collision produced enough heat to melt the entire globe. Once Earth melted, its elements rearranged themselves according to density. The most dense elements formed the planet's core. There, radioactive decay generated enough heat to convert Earth's interior into molten rock. Moderately dense elements floated to the surface, much as fat floats to the top of hot chicken soup. These elements ultimately cooled to form a solid crust.[1]

[1] Ibid

The new large lump of planetary material had to be struck to be melted. And once melted, it was miraculously able to rearrange to form today's concentric planetary structure. And all this happened because of a collision with another planet sized object, which raises the following question. Why did this collision cause Earth to melt? Why did it not just smash both new planets into new asteroids? The coincidence is remarkable, and coincidental. The problem for such evolutionary cosmologists is this. They have a theory of how large planet sized objects could be formed by gravity, but this theory does not explain current structure, so they have had to make up a story to explain it. Yet the story is not based on any observation. Planet sized objects do not collide to cause heat and melting. Yet the impossible is deemed to happen, because a naturalistic explanation is required for philosophical reasons.

About 4 billion years ago, Earth cooled enough to allow the first solid rocks to form on its surface. For millions of years afterwards, violent volcanic activity shook Earth's crust.[1]

Notice in the last quoted sentence above that the concept of conjecture has been abandoned. Students are being told that the

violent volcanic shaking is an established fact, when it is not. Once again, the impossible is deemed possible, because of the scale of deep time.

About 3.8 billion years ago, Earth's surface cooled enough for water to remain a liquid. Thunderstorms drenched the planet, and oceans covered much of the surface. Those primitive oceans were brown because they contained lots of dissolved iron. The earliest sedimentary rocks, which were deposited in water, have been dated to this period. This was the Earth on which life appeared.

The thunderstorms are convenient, because, as we shall see, they provide a source of electricity for a planetary version of the Miller-Urey Experiment, though, in practice, there would be nowhere near enough electrical energy. How could sedimentary rocks be dated to this period? It would not be by radiometric dating, which is used on igneous, not sedimentary, rocks. Well, the sedimentary rocks are so dated, because this is the era when they must have formed. The argument is, in fact, circular. Once again, we have a long breakfast of 3.8 billion years, during which the impossible becomes possible.

For several reasons, atoms do not assemble themselves into complex

---

[1] Ibid, p424

organic molecules or living cells on Earth today.[1]

This is, of course, a remarkable admission. It is a clear admission that the process, which they will go on to describe using the Miller-Urey Experiment, is, in fact, impossible. Their answer to this problem is to use a fuzzy word construction - the Unanswered Question!

But the early Earth was a very different place. Could organic molecules have evolved under those conditions?

The answer to the unanswered question is obviously assumed to be "Yes", but, in fact, depends on your definition of organic molecules. We are going to see a clear case of bait and switch being set up. Let me ask a question of my own. What is an organic molecule? Well, it is a molecule of an organic compound. So, what is an organic compound? One might popularly suppose that it is a compound necessary for life, and that, indeed, is how the term was originally used. Today, however, the term organic compound applies merely to a compound containing at least carbon and hydrogen, where there are two or more carbon atoms joined in a chain. All molecules from living things are organic compounds, but most organic compounds are not found in living things, or even produced from them. Many organic compounds are produced from abiotic material, and play no part in the chemistry of living things at all.

So, into this confusion this Biology text book introduces the Miller-Urey Experiment. It is possible that many of you are very familiar with this experiment, but I had better explain it for those who are not.

In the 1950s, Stanley Miller and Harold Urey wanted to see if life could be produced under laboratory conditions from non-life. So they set up apparatus, as shown. The reaction chamber would contain gases, simulating what Miller and Urey determined must have been the Earth's "primitive" atmosphere, with such gases as ammonia, methane, and water vapor. Electric sparks were introduced to the gaseous reactants. The mixture was then condensed, and the reactants removed for analysis. The flask of products contained a mixture of amino acids. The Prentice Hall Biology text book says this about the products.

Miller and Urey produced amino acids, which are needed to make proteins, by passing sparks through a mixture of hydrogen, methane, ammonia, and water... Miller and Urey's experiments suggested how mixtures of the organic compounds necessary for life could have

---

[1] Ibid

arisen from simpler compounds present on a primitive Earth.[1]

This is, of course, disingenuous. A number of inconvenient observations must be made.

1. It is true that amino acids were produced. However, we have already noted the absence of elemental oxygen, because the text notes that this would have destroyed the nascent amino acids molecules. Therefore, the reason for the choice of reactant gases is dependant on the products required, which actually invalidates the experiment as a circular argument.

2. Only about 20 amino acids are actually required for life. This experiment does not produce the "required" mixture of amino acids.

3. Amino acids contain carbon atoms, to which four different groups are attached. The four bonds on the

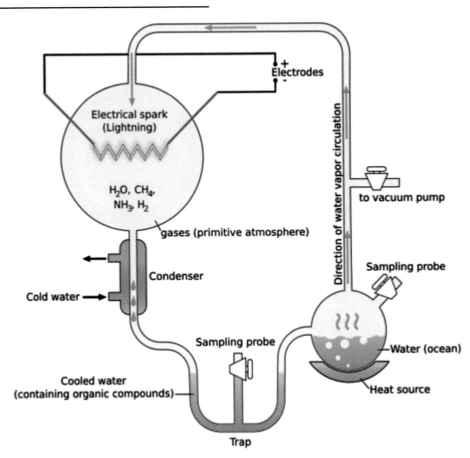

The famous Miller-Urey experim,ent: Public domain drawing, Wikipedia Commons

carbon atoms are arranged tetrahedrally, meaning that each molecule can exist in two mirror images, referred to as "left" and "right", depending on their rotational effect on plane polarized light. This experiment produces a 50-50 mixture of left and right forms. This is known as a racemic mixture. But compounds in living organisms contain exclusively left-handed amino acids.

---

[1] Ibid

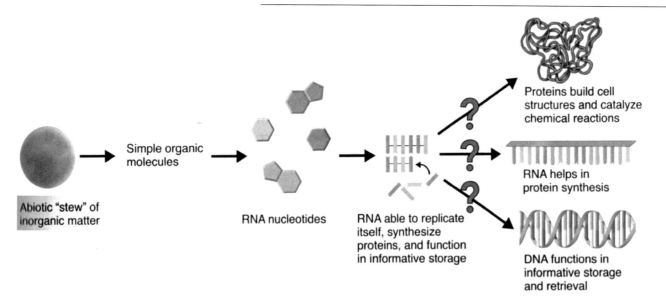

Abiotic "stew" of inorganic matter

Simple organic molecules

RNA nucleotides

RNA able to replicate itself, synthesize proteins, and function in informative storage

Proteins build cell structures and catalyze chemical reactions

RNA helps in protein synthesis

DNA functions in informative storage and retrieval

4. There are also some simpler objections. Where, for example, is the chemical trap in the ocean, that could isolate the products, preventing them from being destroyed by re-entering the reaction chamber.

The text book proceeds to admit that the original experiment was inaccurate, and goes on to claim, without evidence, that better results have been obtained with different "early atmospheres". However, their confidence is undermined by their flow chart, suggesting how living cells could have developed from such an abiotic "stew". The diagram, reproduced here, refers to information being stored in RNA and DNA, but does not explain how random processes could encode such information. In fact, information science shows that information does not depend on the medium, through which it is stored. This important principle will be explained in more detail later. The whole of this section is trying to explain how complex DNA could come about by chance. Not only do they fail to explain this, they leave gaping holes in their evolutionary explanations, which can only be filled by their resorting to impossible things becoming possible, given deep time.

It may be commented by some that my criticisms of this book's text on this subject is unfair, for the following reason. It is surely not possible for students to learn the full depth of this topic all that once. In chemistry and physics also, students learn concepts in simpler environments first, before they can learn greater subtleties. But such a criticism would be disingenuous. The text is suggesting that processes happen, which are contrary to principles that the students would learn at the same level in chemistry or physics. This contradiction is simply covered up, by pretending to the student that more education or research will help explain further. This can be seen clearly, as the textbook authors try to answer the question "How Did Life Begin?". This they begin with an important admission.

> *A stew of organic molecules is a long way from a living cell, and this leap from nonlife to life is the greatest gap in scientific theories of Earth's early history.*[1]

Read what Miller and Levine say about DNA and RNA formation.

> *Another unanswered question... is the origin of DNA ad RNA. Remember that all cells are controlled by information stored in DNA, which is transcribed into RNA and then translated into proteins... Under the right conditions, some RNA sequences can help DNA replicate.*

The circularity of their argument is clear. RNA is encoded by DNA. DNA is replicated by RNA. Which is first? And if the right conditions can cause this to happen, what are those conditions?

> *A series of experiments that simulated conditions of the early Earth have suggested that small sequences of RNA could have formed and replicated on their own.*

Why do the authors not describe these experiments? Why are there no references to the literature on these experiments? It is because no such RNAs have been made and self-replicated. Their get-out clause is the use of the word "suggested". How does an experiment suggest anything? Experiments do not suggest. They show. It is the interpretation which suggests. It is possible to observe an experiment that produces amino acids and conclude that this experiment *suggests* that RNA replication might be possible.

> *From this relatively simple RNA-based form of life, several steps could have led to the system of DNA-directed protein synthesis that exists now.*

What are these several steps? Once again, we must emphasize that students of this level, using equivalent age-appropriate chemistry textbooks, will see, if permitted to do so, that the steps involve are chemically and thermodynamically impossible. Wool is being pulled over their eyes. It is important for students to question everything, because such questioning is good science. I would add a brief word of caution at this point. Obviously, there are examples in science education where it is not possible to give all

---

[1] Ibid, p425

the fine details of information to a student immediately. There is sometimes a case for saying that something can be explained better in a year or two when the student has more knowledge. So, what we are specifically looking for here is where the wording is deliberately woolly, to cover over processes which are impossible, but are assumed to become possible, if left for millions of years.

Case Study: Cosmology

It is not only in the realm of biology where magic words are used, and impossible things involved before breakfast. In a cosmological breakfast, the timescale is measured, not in millions of years, but in billions. This is deep, deep time.

The principle "evolutionary" cosmology in vogue today is the Big Bang Theory. Actually, the term "Big Bang" was originally a term of abuse, coined by an opponent of the theory, but, as happens in such cases, it is now the accepted nomenclature for the idea that all matter, energy, and space in the universe was once part of a singularity, which "exploded" (it is not said to be an actual explosion), so that all material spread out. The Big Bang Theory is a great deal more complex than many suppose, and it is in the midst of

some of these complications that the magic words appear. Indeed, the very concept of singularity is a magic word. How can we imagine a point, where there is zero volume, yet infinite density? The infinite density part is mathematically logical, since any finite mass divided by zero volume will give infinite density. However, the practical outworking of this is beyond what our minds can comprehend. Maybe it is so incomprehensible precisely because it is really a sophisticated magic word concept.

Further than that, no one can really properly explain where this singularity came from. There is insistent talk from many astrophysicists about quantum changes, but this would also appear to be a form of magic words. Consider the following statements.

It was a "nothing" so profound it defies human comprehension.[1]

This does not read like a scientific statement. However, it is only a comment out of context, so we had better examine some similar quotes.

Our Universe probably came into existence not only from nothing, but from nowhere.[2]

[1] Couper, H. & Henbest, N. (1997), *Big Bang,* (London: DK Publishing), p8

[2] Ibid, p9

Brad Lemley has more to say on the subject of nothingness.

> *To the average person it might seem obvious that nothing can happen in nothing. But to a quantum physicist, nothing is, in fact, something.*[1]

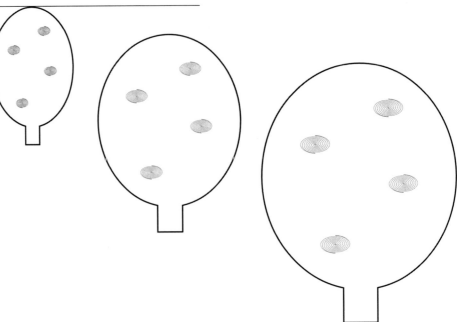

Balloons and Expanding Universe

The key phrase is "nothing is, in fact, something". This is certainly a mouth-stopper of a statement. Don't interrupt my cosmology lesson, sunshine; nothing is, in fact, something! The student is supposed to accept such a statement, because it comes with the authority of a quantum physicist, and they know magic words that you can dream of. After all, young man, you are just an "average person", not a high priest, I mean quantum physicist.

Lemley again:

> *Quantum theory also holds that a vacuum, like atoms, is subject to quantum uncertainties. This means that things can materialise out of the vacuum, although they tend to vanish back into it*

quickly....this phenomenon has never been observed directly...[2]

Science is about observation and repetition. Things do not just materialize out of nothing. Even Lemley admits that no one has ever seen it happen. It is, after all, impossible. But impossible things can happen, given millions of years, or the impossible can happen if it involves a quantum process.

"I have in my hand an invisible cabbage."

"But I can't see it!"

"Of course you can't see it. It's invisible. If you could see it, then it would not be invisible.

Of course, many people will assume, from reading my comments, that I do not understand the physics involved. I do. I was

---

[1] Lemley, B., *Guth's Grand Guess*, Discover (**23**), April 2002, p35

[2] Ibid, p38

a teacher of physics and chemistry in government schools in Britain for nearly 20 years, and I taught this topic many times. Yet the implications are profound. None of these events are actually possible, but we have to pretend that they happen in this quantum universe, so that we can explain existence without God.

Tipler and Barrow's Anthropic Principle places humanity back at the center of the universe. Picture from Dollar Photo Club, royalty paid.

Critics of the Big Bang Theory have pointed out that the very existence of our current universe is impossible, if we started from a singularity. The Cosmological Principle suggests that all points in the universe are equivalent. The universe looks much the same, whichever way we look at it, and whichever way we travel. To explain this complex idea, some have suggested imagining a 2D universe, which is actually printed on the surface of a large balloon. As the balloon is inflated, the galaxies on its surface get gradually farther apart, yet none is in a special, or unique position.

Yet cosmologists cannot explain how a singularity could produce a universe with galaxies. The early expansion of the universe would require that there be no irregularities within it. Yet it is precisely these irregularities that are needed to explain the galaxies. Williamson and Hartnett put it as follows:

> *Only if the balloon (the model of the universe) has a weak spot or is punctured does the rubber collapse. In a similar manner, if the big-bang universe had no "weak spots" and it were not to be "punctured" by a center, then it would remain in an uncollapsed state. However, the early universe needs to have small irregularities in it that can later produce the galaxies, so the perfect smoothness required to avoid collapse into a singularity is incompatible with the existence of the galaxies. These*

irregularities act like "weak spots" and "punctures" in the balloon analogy, and collapse occurs irrespective of whether there is a center or not.[1]

So, it is beginning to look like even the concept of the primordial singularity is a magic word, to explain something that cannot possibly happen.

John D. Barrow and Frank Tipler have suggested an alternative to the Cosmological Principle, because of the vagaries involved in understanding the concept of the primordial singularity. Their alternative is known as the *Anthropic Principle*. The Cosmological Principle suggests that there is no reason for the universe to exist. It is simply a random, chance, quantum fluctuation. The Anthropic Principle, by contrast, suggests that it is not possible for the Big Bang and other processes to have arisen by chance. A Christian might be tempted to shout "Hallelujah!" Indeed, Barrow was awarded the Templeton Proze in 2006 - a prize awarded to people who have "made an exceptional contribution to affirming life's spiritual dimension, whether through insight, discovery, or practical works"[2]. However, general rejoicing by Christians would be premature. The god suggested by the Anthropic Principle is not really God, but merely an extrapolation of certain formulae and observations. Michael Frayn has described the Anthropic Principle thus:

It's this simple paradox. The Universe is very old and very large. Humankind, by comparison, is only a tiny disturbance in one small corner of it - and a very recent one. Yet the Universe is only very large and very old because we are here to say it is... And yet, of course, we all know perfectly well that it is what it is whether we are here or not.[3]

This is a version of the suggestion that "evolution had to happen, because here we are!". Such a statement is a circular argument. It "proves" evolution only if evolution is assumed to be true.

Summary

Magic words are words or phrases used to describe phenomena which are actually impossible. But they are assumed to have occurred, if enough time has elapsed for the event, or if some unusual process has caused it to happen. In many cases, evolutionists make an unwarranted appeal to authority, in order to try to prevent their readers and students noticing that

[1] Williams, A. & Hartnett, J. (2005), *Dismantling the Big Bang*, (Green Forest, AR: 2005), p100

[2] < http://www.templetonprize.org >, retrieved 7/2/2015

[3] Frayn, M. (2006), *The Human Touch: Our Part in the Creation of a Universe*, (London: Faber)

magic words are being used. You are left to assume that you are ignorant if you suggest that something is impossible, because, if you knew better, you would know that anything can happen given enough time! Not!

If something is impossible now, then millions of years do not make it possible.

I am reminded of a scene in Douglas Adams' second book in his *Hitchhikers' Guide to the Galaxy* series.

The Restaurant at the End of the Universe is one of the most extraordinary ventures in the entire history of catering.

It is built on the fragmented ruins of an eventually ruined planet which is enclosed in a vast time bubble and projected forward in time to the precise moment of the End of the Universe.

This is, many would say, impossible.

In it, guests take their places at table and eat sumptuous meals while watching the whole of creation explode around them.

This, many would say, is equally impossible.

You can arrive for any sitting you like without prior reservation because you can book retrospectively, as it were, when returning to your own time.

This is, many would now insist, absolutely impossible.

At the Restaurant you can meet and dine with a fascinating cross-section of the entire population of space and time.

This, it can be explained patiently, is also impossible.

You can visit it as many times as you like and be sure of never meeting yourself, because of the embarrassment this usually causes.

This, even if the rest were true, which it isn't, is patently impossible, say the doubters.

All you have to do is deposit one penny in a savings account in your own era, and when you arrive at the End of Time the operation of compund interest means that the fabulous cost of your meal has been paid for.

This, many claim, is not merely impossible but clearly insane, which is why the advertising executives of the star system of Bastablon came up with this slogan: "If you've done six impossible things this morning, why not round it off

with breakfast at Milliways, the

Restaurant at the End of the Universe?"[1]

---

[1] Adams, D. (1995), *The Restaurant at the End of the Universe*, (Del Ray)

Chapter 4

WORLDVIEWS

Everybody has a worldview. Everybody has a presupposition. But many people do not realize that they do.

Many creationists have been asked for evidence that creation happened as it says in the Bible, or evidence that the Bible is true. They have requested that this evidence be neutral. Now, I have a presupposition that God exists and that the Bible is true. Therefore, I interpret every piece of evidence through this filter. In a radio discussion program on BBC radio some years ago, Richard Dawkins said of me "every point this man makes, he always quotes the Bible." It was not meant as a compliment, but I took it as one. The point that so many, including so many Christians, fail to understand is that everyone has a presupposition. In order to find step off my presupposition that the Bible is true, I have to adopt a line of reasoning, into which the Bible is not relevant. This is not a neutral position at all. It is a highly presuppositional position.

Creationists too, however, fall foul at this juncture. Because evidence has been demanded of them, they seek to provide that evidence. They are searching for the silver bullet that will prove evolution wrong and creation right. But it is my

Evidence is normally presented in court. Picture of "Old Bailey" by Thomas Rowlandson and Augustus Pugin, Public Domain

"In the beginning, God created..." Photo by NASA, Public Domain

presenting evidence for the creation of the world, then the skeptic is again the judge, and is being asked to declare whether or not the words of God are true or not. Neither of these scenarios are worthy activities for the Christian, when we understand them in this context.

The Bible knows nothing of this approach. Nowhere do we read in the Bible an essay giving the cogent arguments for and against the existence of God, and asking the readers to make an informed judgment.

contention that this approach is fundamentally flawed.

Where is evidence normally presented? In normal experience, evidence is typically presented in a court of law. The evidence is presented to the judge (and the jury, in some cases) in order to try to persuade them of the veracity of your case. If you are presenting evidence for the existence of God, then who is the judge? You are turning the atheist into the judge, and asking him to pronounce on the veracity of your case that God exists. If you are

Rather, the Bible begins with the words "In the beginning, God created the heavens and the earth." It assumes that the existence of God, and the veracity of His words, is a reasonable and obvious position to take. Indeed, the only comment the Bible makes on the possible non-existence of God is a single phrase in Psalms, considered so important that it is repeated, and is found in Psalm 14:1 and again in Psalm 53:1.

The fool has said in his heart, "There is no God."

Sometimes, people get upset when I point this fact out. "Are you calling me a fool?", the skeptic might ask. The answer to this is clear. No, I am not calling you a fool. The Bible calls you a fool.

To attempt to provide neutral evidence for the existence of God is impossible. In fact, the skeptic does not start from a neutral position. He starts from the assumption that evidence is independent, and stands on no basis. This is not, in fact, the case. As the educationalist Mark Roques put it:

Science, be it chemistry, physics or biology, is always practised in the light of a person's worldview.[1]

[1] Roques, M., *Curriculum Unmasked*, Towards a

Picture courtesy of Answers in Genesis

An analogy that I like to use is that of geometry. In a geometric proof, it is not necessary to prove that two parallel lines will never meet. This point is assumed. It is an axiom, and is based on one of Euclid's five axioms. It is possible to envisage non-Euclidian geometries, with different axioms, but the axioms are still necessary. In the same way, it is possible for one to start a philosophy with presuppositions other than Christian presuppositions, but it is not possible to do without presuppositions. Even a statement to the effect that there are no presuppositions would be logically self-defeating as that would be a presuppositional

Christian Understanding of Education, (Monarch, 1989), p153

Picture courtesy of Answers in Genesis

statement. In our discussions with skeptics, therefore, it should not be our position that we would temporarily abandon our presupposition to stand on that of the skeptic. Rather we show that our presupposition is the only reasonable one, from which all explanations flow, and from which evidence makes sense.

In our discussions with skeptics, creationists have sometimes given the impression that the requirement is to find two piles of evidence; one for creation and one for evolution. We can then compare the

The whole subject of presuppositions is big. For that reason, I already have a book drafted on the subject of Presuppositional Apologetics, which is called *Only Believe.* God willing, this book will be published early in 2016, so I will leave the detailed discussion of that subject for that book. In

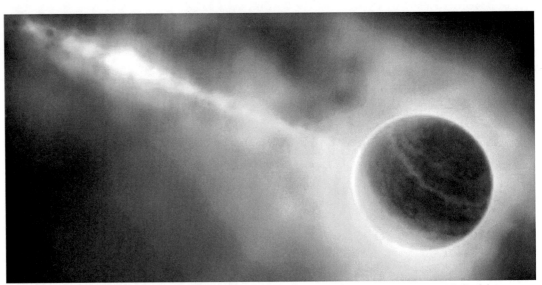

The formation of a giant gas planet (right) near the star HD 100546 (left) is not yet complete, allowing astronomers to observe the process.

evidence in each pile and decide whose evidence is the more persuasive. The fallacy of this position can be understood when we consider the use of fossil evidence by both creationists and evolutionists. Both sides claim that fossil evidence supports their position. But if we look at a fossil, can we really classify it as a creationist fossil or an evolutionary fossil? Of course not! It is just a fossil. What is at stake is how that fossil is interpreted, according to the differing presuppositions.

brief, however, it is the contention of the presuppositional apologist that the existence of knowledge and the laws of science, logic and morality only make sense when we start from the presupposition that God exists and that the Bible is true. The paradox is that in order to criticize a biblical worldview, it turns out that the atheist has to borrow ideas from the biblical worldview itself!

So a biblical presupposition is a good thing. However, since it is our contention that there is no neutral starting point, it means that there must be negative starting points. The job of this chapter is to show when scientific articles, textbooks and TV programs are using an incorrect presupposition or worldview, without realizing it.

Case Study: Science Daily

The website Science Daily[1] is actually a very good website. There are many interesting articles on science and technology written in a popular easy-to-understand style. I am glad the website exists. However, in common with so many popular science publishers, their articles are heavily influenced by evolutionary ideas. I frequently find articles that illustrate ideas included in my chapters on fuzzy words and magic words. There are also some examples of worldview confusion, appropriate to this chapter.

Take, as an example, a article published on July 1st 2015, entitled *Observing the Birth of*

Artist's impression of a near star gas giant. Public domain

a Planet.[2] The introduction makes the following claim:

> *Astronomers have confirmed the existence of a young giant gas planet still embedded in the midst of the disk of gas and dust surrounding its parent star. For the first time, scientists are able to directly study the formation of a planet at a very early stage.*

There is a fair amount of worldview bias in this article. The trick is to make sure that our own bias is not involved in our designation of evolutionary worldview bias.

---

[1] < http://www.sciencedaily.com >

[2] *Observing the Birth of a Planet,* < http://www.sciencedaily.com/releases/2015/07/150701114809.htm >, July 1st 2015, accessed July 3rd 2015

In this case, it is very easy to spot the pure bias. For example, we are told that "a young giant gas planet" has been found. It is worth remembering that no planet sized object has actually been seen. Its presence is inferred from observations of effects elsewhere. Now look at the fascinating phrase "still embedded in the midst of the disk of gas and dust surrounding its parent star. Even secular evolutionists do not all agree that planets were formed by gravitational accretion of dust from a disk of gas. Yet the existence and history of such a process is assumed by this article to be proven. They can therefore state that this observation has been "confirmed". Moreover, we read that "scientists are able to directly study the formation of a planet at a very early stage." This is disingenuous. Does anyone know how long they expect the birth of a planet to take? The truth is that these astronomers are not witnessing the formation of a planet. They are witnessing a interesting phenomenon, whose happening has coincided with news reports. These reports are being interpreted, with reference to a clear worldview bias. No accretion of dust and gas into this planet has been observed. The dust is there, and the planet is possibly there. The rest is presuppositional.

HRH The Prince of Wales, Prince Charles
Photo from Wikimedia Commons

Case Study: HRH The Prince of Wales

In 2010, His Royal Highness The Prince of Wales published a major work, titled *Harmony*. This book - widely assumed to be a sort-of manifesto for Prince Charles's future reign - argues for an awareness and implementation of a Gaian-style interdependency. Prince Charles's book contains a great deal that is presuppositional, in a negative way. Consider the following, which is a description of ice core extraction:

The further the drill went down, the older the ice it extracted, at the bottom pulling up samples more than 800,000 years old. The ice drill thus enables us to look back over the best part of a million years and so in a way is a time-travel machine.[1]

There are a number of unproven statements here, which stem straight from Prince Charles's presuppositions. Michael Oard has shown that the traditional uniformitarian interpretation of ice cores is flawed, due to worldview assumptions.

The assumed thickness of the annual layers is important because it determines how many measurements of each variable are made down the length of the core. Based on their expected annual thickness, uniformitarian scientists take enough measurements to resolve what they believe are annual cycles. For oxygen isotope oscillations, they normally need eight measurements per annual cycle to pick up the 'annual' signature. However, from oxygen isotope measurements they were only able to resolve annual layers in the GISP2 core down to about 300 m although annual layers have supposedly been identified at significantly deeper levels in other

Greenland cores. So they have used other variables, such as cloudy bands, electrical conductivity, laser-light scattered from dust, major ion chemistry, and volcanic ash bands, to establish the 'annual' layers. Significantly, their interpretation of annual layers from these variables has been determined by the thickness of the annual layers that they expect, based on their model.[2]

Therefore, Prince Charles's assertions that lower ice is older ice, that the lower samples were 800,000 years old, that the ice drill allows for a million years, and that it is a type of time machine are all invalid. These statements of time are not being used as *magic words*, as we saw in the previous chapter. They are errors based entirely on a faulty worldview.

Case Study: Adaptive Radiation

Adaptive Radiation is a common device used in high school textbooks to convince the student of evolution. It often accompanies the classic bait-and-switch confusion between Darwinian evolution and speciation. Let us look at these concepts in turn.

Adaptive radiation is a sort-of family-tree diagram, showing how groups of

[1] HRH The Prince of Wales (2010), *Harmony*, (London: Harper Collins), p33

[2] Oard, M.J. (2001), *Do Greenland ice cores show over one hundred thousand years of annual layers?*, Journal of Creation 15(3):39–42, December 2001

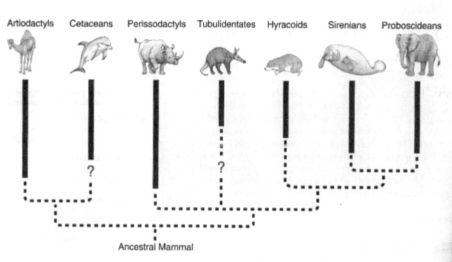

Miller, K. And Levine, J. (2002), Biology, (Upper Saddle River, NJ: Pearson Education Inc), 2002 edition, p436, Figure 17-22, used under "Fair-use".

rearrangement or loss of genetic information in the development of new species within a kind. Evolutionists (such as Miller and Levine) unjustifiably extrapolate this to a *macroevolutionary* scenario. Yet this latter involves the changing of animals from one kind to another, and requires the spontaneous creation of new genetic information - something which is never observed. With these considerations stated, let us examine what Miller and Levine say.

animals are supposed to have evolved from common ancestors. This tree will have branches, because we are particularly looking at common ancestry.

In the textbook quoted in a previous chapter, Miller and Levine use the bait-and-switch confusion. They point to the genuinely observed adaptation of finches in the Galapagos, as observed by Charles Darwin. This adaptive radiation, however, shows finches turning into finches. Creationists used to refer to this form of adaptation as *microevolution*, but it is best not to involke the term evolution at all. We prefer the term *speciation*. Speciation invlves the

Often, studies of fossils or of living organisms show that a single species or a small group of species has evolved into several different forms that live in

Galápagos Islands Finches						
Shape of Head and Beak						
Common Name of Finch Species	Vegetarian tree finch	Large insectivorous tree finch	Woodpecker finch	Cactus ground finch	Sharp-beaked ground finch	Large ground finch
Main Food	Fruit	Insects	Insects	Cactus	Seeds	Seeds
Feeding Adaptation	Parrotlike beak	Grasping beak	Uses cactus spines	Large crushing beak	Pointed crushing beak	Large crushing beak
Habitat	Trees	Trees	Trees	Ground	Ground	Ground

Miller, K. And Levine, J. (2002), Biology, (Upper Saddle River, NJ: Pearson Education Inc), 2002 edition, p406, Figure 16-13, used under "Fair-use".

different ways. This process is known as **adaptive radiation**. You have already learned about the adaptive radiation of Darwin's finches. In that case, more than a dozen species evolved from a single species.

The relative sizes of large mammals. Photo by author

Adaptive radiations can also occur on a much larger scale. Dinosaurs, for example, were the products of a spectacular adaptive radiation among ancient reptiles. The first dinosaurs and the earliest mammals evolved at about the same time. Dinosaurs and other ancient reptiles, however,

underwent an adaptive radiation first and "ruled" Earth for about 150 million years. During that time, mammals remained small and relatively scarce. But the disappearance of the dinosaurs cleared the way for the great adaptive radiation of mammals. This radiation, part of which is shown in **Figure 17-22**, produced the great diversity of mammals in the Cenozoic.[1]

Because Miller and Levine's Figure 17-22 is important to their argument, I have reproduced it here under "fair-use" terms. Because Darwin's finches have been mentioned, I have also reproduced Miller and Levine's figure 16-13, which compares these finches. It needs to be stated again and again that Darwin was right about these finches. It is clear that they had a

[1] Miller, K. And Levine, J. (2002), *Biology*, (Upper Saddle River, NJ: Pearson Education Inc), 2002 edition, p436

Mesonychid (with my reflection). Photo by author

dotted lines indicate lines of conjecture. It is important to notice that every single junction on this adaptive radiation diagram - and, for that matter, all other such evolutionary adaptive radiation diagrams - all consist of conjecture, rather than actual fossil evidence.

common ancestor, which was also a finch. This does not involve the spontaneous generation of new genetic information. It is not comparing like with like to suggest that this gives evidence for the mammalian adaptive radiation diagram.

One of the most significant observations to make on the mammalian adaptive radiation diagram is the difference between solid lines and dotted lines joining these animals. The solid lines represent actual fossil evidence. This is important, because some of the solid lines are longer than others, indicating that evolutionists believe they have been around for longer, as there must be fossil evidence contained in lower strata of the geologic column. The

Evolution of the Whale Display

One of the important subplots included in the BBC/PBS documentary series, Walking with Prehistoric Beasts, was that of the evolution of the whale. It is assumed by evolutionists that the whale, being a mammal, must have evolved from a land animal. As is usual in such cases, a large number of progenitors are proposed. But some of the most interesting names

The Evolution of the Whale. Photo by author

suggested are the *basilosaurus* ("king lizard"), *ambulocetus* ("walking whale"), and *mesonychid* ("middle claw"). London's Natural History Museum has a fine display of whale evolution, notable for its excellent quality of exhibit, and also the clear use of worldview bias in the language used in its displays.

A very large room in the NHM houses a number of full-size models of mammals. This is especially helpful, as it gives visitors a perspective on the relative sizes of hippos, elephants and whales - especially the hugeness of the great baleen whales, such as the blue whale.

Climbing to the mezzanine overlooking this large mammal gallery, we find an exhibition on whale evolution. The first display features the mesonychid, and gives details on what they think it was like and how they think it behaved. Leaving aside the conjectural nature of the behavior for a moment, it does seem apparent that the creature resembled a dog or wolf. The mesonychid display is labeled with the following text.

Mesonyx ("middle claw") is the type genus of the family Mesonychidae, *the type family of the Order* Mesonychia *(sometimes referred to by its older name, "Acreodi"), an order that may have been ancestral to cetaceans.*

The purpose of the entire exhibit is to show the evolution of the whale from these dog-like land animals. So, the Natural History Museum provides its "proof" in the form of a tale of three skulls. The case holds three skulls, deliberately arranged to illustrate whale evolution. The first skull belongs to a mesonychid, and has two nostrils near the end of its snout. The second shows an ambulocetus, with two nostrils halfway along its snout. The third shows a "modern" whale, with a single nostril, or blowhole, on top of its skull. The clear implication of the display is that we are viewing a near-linear evolution, in which the fossils are arranged in order of age.

There is, however, a problem. The fossil ambulocetus is older, according to evolutionary dating, than the mesonychid. This is embarrassing, but easily solved. Looking at the time displays beneath the glass case, we see that the evolutionists believe that this particular fossil ambulocetus was one of the first of its kind, while this particular mesonychid is one of the last of its kind. Therefore, the existence of these species overlaps. Therefore, they can display the fossils in the correct evolutionary order.

But what justification do they have for supposing that the mesonychid is a late example of its type? Simply that they "know" it must have evolved into an ambulocetus, or similar. In other words, they had to use the Theory of Evolution in order to construct this display, which they then offer as "proof" of evolution. This is, of course, an example of the logical fallacy known as "circular reasoning". This use of presuppositional circular reasoning is common in evolutionary arguments.

Summary and Conclusions

It is possible that readers may find these worldview words a bit more difficult to spot than the fuzzy words or the magic words. They are nonetheless very important. What we have seen is that many examples of popular science use concepts, which are not free-standing. They are dependent entirely upon the author's worldview. Although creationists also use arguments based on their worldview, the difference is that we are aware and up front about so doing. The characteristic of the phrases that I am helping you to identify is that they are used to conceal. Statements are made, which assume a worldview position, which cannot be justified.

Chapter 5

HAMLET AND HUMPTY DUMPTY

Isn't the use of language fascinating? The very way in which speakers and writers sharpen the tools of their trade can, at one and the same time, both confuse and elucidate meaning. Language is the only means we have to transfer thoughts from one person to another. But the download and upload of information is not perfect. It is applied with nuances and personality. How often has one person delivered a hard truth to me, which I won't accept, then another delivers the same message, using pretty much the same words, and that I do accept, because, rightly or wrongly, my respect for the second person is higher than for the first?

Information is transmitted by the medium of words. Yet the use of words may not give a full meaning. For example, suppose you look at a word cloud of my book, *The Six Days of Genesis.* Word clouds give a certain amount of information. The greater the size of the font used in the cloud, the more times that word is used. Therefore, you could look at this word cloud and determine that words like Genesis, God and six are used a great deal in the book. That gives you some information about its content. But the word cloud is still not a substitute for actually reading the book. This is the same in everyday language. Words may convey a certain amount of meaning, but no further.

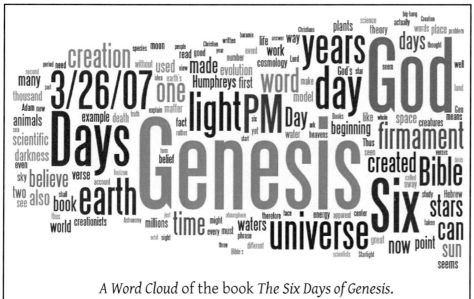

A Word Cloud of the book The Six Days of Genesis.

What Does the Bible Say about Language?

The Bible actually has a great deal to say about language. It will therefore be useful to conduct a quick paper trail of verses throughout the Bible on this subject.

Look first a the language of the first verse of John's Gospel.

Opening of John's Gospel

> *In the beginning was the Word, and the Word was with God, and the Word was God.*

It would appear that the phrase "in the beginning" is important. In English, this phrase is reminiscent of the first phrase of the Bible - Genesis 1:1. But we have to remember that the Old Testament was written in Hebrew and the New in Greek, so we had better dig further before we conclude that the phrases are the same. Look, for example, at the Majority Text for John 1:1.

Ἐν ἀρχῇ ἦν ὁ Λόγος, καὶ ὁ Λόγος ἦν πρὸς τὸν Θεόν, καὶ Θεὸς ἦν ὁ Λόγος.

The phrase translated "in the beginning" is *Εν ἀρχη*. Now, let's look at Genesis 1:1.

> *In the beginning God created the heavens and the earth.*

The Hebrew will not actually help us at this point, so let's look at the Septuagint (LXX), a Greek translation of the Old Testament, made a couple of hundred years before Christ.

Ἐν ἀρχῇ ἐποίησεν ὁ θεὸς τὸν οὐρανὸν καὶ τὴν γῆν.

Even those without any Greek knowledge can see that the same phrase is used. In fact, the Greek phrase, *Εν ἀρχη (en arche)*, is used only to refer to the beginning of the whole of creation. Therefore, it is clear that the opening words of John's Gospel really and truly are meant to refer back to Genesis. From this analysis, we conclude that the Word (Λογος, logos), which John makes clear is a direct reference to Jesus Christ, was there at the Creation, and before, and was actually responsible for creating.

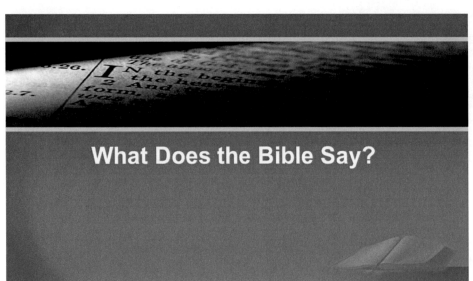

What Does the Bible Say?

Words Are Important

My son, give attention to my words; Incline your ear to my sayings. Proverbs 4:20

To understand meaning, there needs to be a level of concentration.

Words Have Meaning

He who has knowledge spares his words, And a man of understanding is of a calm spirit. Even a fool is counted wise when he holds his peace; When he shuts his lips, he is considered perceptive. Proverbs 17:27-28.

I have often thought that Solomon had a sense of humor with some of these proverbs. This humor is more evident in the New Living Translation.

A truly wise person uses few words; a person with understanding is even-tempered. Even fools are thought wise when they keep silent; with their mouths shut, they seem intelligent. Proverbs 17:27-28 NLT.

I love the phrase "with their mouths shut, they seem intelligent"!

Words Can Be Deceptive

Now this I say lest anyone should deceive you with persuasive words. Colossians 2:4

If anyone teaches otherwise and does not consent to wholesome words, even the words of our Lord Jesus Christ, and to the doctrine which accords with godliness, he is proud, knowing nothing, but is obsessed with disputes and arguments over words, from which come envy, strife, reviling, evil suspicions, useless wranglings of men of corrupt minds and destitute of the truth, who suppose that godliness is a means of gain. From such withdraw yourself. 1 Timothy 6:3-5.

Not a great deal of comment is needed on these verses. I am sure that many of you reading this will be familiar with the sort if people described in these verses. Deceivers will use words in order to carry out their deceptions. These deceptions are not always obvious; otherwise they would not be deceptions. We see that deceptions are achieved by persuasive words, unwholesome words, proud words, and useless wranglings. Paul instructs Timothy not to be associated with such people.

Sound Words Develop Faith

Hold fast the pattern of sound words which you have heard from me, in faith and love which are in Christ Jesus. 2 Timothy 1:13

On the positive side, words can have good uses. Here, we are told that we need to hold to "sound words". The word

translated as "sound" is actually ὑγιαίνω - (*hugiainō*), from which we get the English word "hygienic". So, Paul is instructing Timothy to use hygienic words, "clean", unsullied words. Our positive words should be carefully chosen, and when we hear negative words from others, we should weigh them carefully, and judge them as such. There is a lot more that could be said on the Bible's use of language, but it can be summarized with the following warning:

Use Words Carefully!

Isaiah 45:18

An fine example of the Bible's careful use of words would be God's declaration about Himself in Isaiah 45:18. Basically, this verse says this:

> *For thus says the LORD, "I am the LORD, and there is no other."*

Use words carefully.

However, there are a number of qualifications, giving us more information about the LORD, before we get to His self-declaration.

> *For thus says the LORD, Who created the heavens, Who is God, Who formed the earth and made it, Who has established it, Who did not create it in vain, Who formed it to be inhabited: "I am the LORD, and there is no other."*

I find it interesting and instructive to split the verse up with structured bullet points, as follows, because I think this brings out the full meaning, as well as the reason for the verse being given.

- *For thus says the LORD,*
  - *Who created the heavens,*
  - *Who is God,*

- *Who formed the earth and made it,*

- *Who has established it,*

- *Who did not create it in vain,*

- *Who formed it to be inhabited:*

• *"I am the LORD, and there is no other."*

Hamlet's Words, Words, Words

If a teacher of English language wants one source above all others to use to illustrate the use of language, it is likely that he or she will turn to Shakespeare.

In Shakespeare's Hamlet, Acts 2 Scene 2, Polonius has been spying on Hamlet. Indeed, he has had his daughter Ophelia engage Hamlet in an artificial conversation. In order to try to avoid suspicion, Hamlet has been feigning madness. In the section, where we are about to jump in, Polonius starts an unusual conversation with the Prince of Denmark.

Polonius. How does my good Lord Hamlet?

Hamlet. Well, God-a-mercy.

Polonius. Do you know me, my lord?

Hamlet. Excellent well. You are a fishmonger.

Later on, Polonius makes a statement that has been adapted into the well-known phrase "there's method in his madness". Strangely, Polonius does not see the significance of Hamlet calling him a fishmonger. Apart from the fact that a fishmonger would be on a much lower social scale than Polonius, and would smell, there is another connotation. In Elizabethan times, the term was a euphemism, almost, though not quite, equivalent to a pimp. Hamlet has presumably chosen his words well. He has just offered a huge insult to Polonius, accusing him of basely using his own daughter to get information, and he has got away with the insult, as Polonius has not understood it. Although this interpretation of the word *fishmonger* is disputed, it seems likely to me, as Hamlet quickly turns the conversation to Ophelia - though he does not let on that he knows anything about Polonius's family.

Polonius. Not I, my lord.

Hamlet. Then I would you were so honest a man.

Polonius. Honest, my lord?

Hamlet. Ay, sir. To be honest, as this world goes, is to be one man

pick'd out of ten thousand.

What do you read, my Lord? Words, words, words. Photo from BBC production, reported on Wikimedia Commons, "fair use"

Polonius. That's very true, my lord.

Hamlet. For if the sun breed maggots in a dead dog, being a god

kissing carrion- Have you a daughter?

Polonius. I have, my lord.

Hamlet. Let her not walk i' th' sun. Conception is a blessing, but not

as your daughter may conceive. Friend, look to't. 1290

Polonius. [aside] How say you by that? Still harping on my daughter. Yet

he knew me not at first. He said I was a fishmonger. He is far

gone, far gone! And truly in my youth I suff'red much extremity

for love- very near this. I'll speak to him again.

It is at this point that the conversation reaches the subject, on which I most want to dwell.

Polonius. What do you read, my lord?

Hamlet. Words, words, words.

Is Hamlet being sarcastic? Of course he is reading words; he could be reading anything else. However, this conversation seems to revolve around the whole subject of the use of language. In two recent filmed versions of this play that I have seen (the first featuring Kenneth Branagh, and the second David ("Doctor Who") Tennant in the title roles), Hamlet is made to twist the words "words, words, words", putting different and unusual emphases on each occurrence. Hamlet's playfulness with language continues with the next exchange.

Polonius. What is the matter, my lord?

Hamlet. Between who?

Polonius. I mean, the matter that you read, my lord.

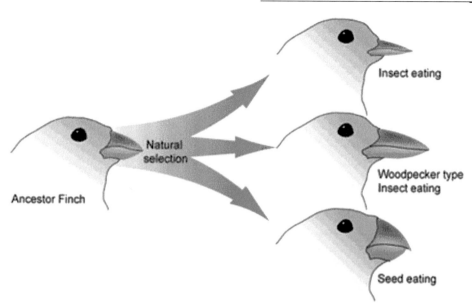

The changes in Darwin's finches was one type of evolution, whereas the change from hypothetical ape-like ancestor to human is another. Both photos are Public Domain, from Wikimedia Commons

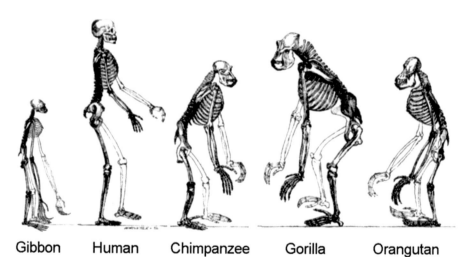

The deliberate miscommunication of seemingly obvious terms seems to me to be common in evolutionary language. In the previous chapter, I referred to bait-and-switch. The last exchange quoted between Polonius and Hamlet is an example of bait-and-switch. Polonius has used one meaning of a technical term, while Hamlet has deliberately substituted another. In the whole analysis of evolutionary language, this is a common source of confusion, and, I have to say, this confusion frequently appears deliberate.

Take, for example, the use of the word *evolution* itself. In its broadest definition, to evolve is simply to change. Anything that has changed has evolved. The creation ministry that I direct has evolved over the years! However, the word *evolution* also refers to more limited types of change. A tadpole changes into a frog. Linguistically, it would be correct to say that the tadpole has evolved into a frog.

When Polonius asks "what is the matter", he is actually enquiring after the subject matter, as he makes clear later. I assume that Hamlet understood this perfectly, and was deliberately feigning ignorance. The recent Tennant production brings this interpretation out.

But biologically, we would not use this term, because evolution in biological terms means something different.

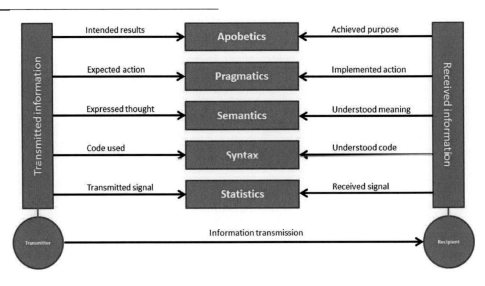

Gitt's Five Levels of Information

Even so, evolutionary biologists are guilty of deliberately confusing two different meanings of the word evolution. What we expect people to mean by evolution is the concept that I would usually call molecules-to-man evolution. This is what is meant when it is stated that apes and humans have a common ancestor. The ape-like common ancestor has changed, over generations, so it is claimed, into a human. Yet the term evolution is sometimes also used to describe the changes found, within a kind, from one species to another. Therefore, the changes in Darwin's finches was one type of evolution, whereas the change from hypothetical ape-like ancestor to human is another. It can be seen that the change from one type of finch to another does not involve making new genetic information. This sort of change is seen in real life, in present-day observational science. However, change from ape-like ancestor to man involves the creation of new genetic information, and this is impossible. So, the two uses of the word *evolution* are not equivalent. In scientific terms, it is preferable to restrict the use of the word evolution to describe the alleged, but impossible, concept of molecules-to-man. For this reason, creationists prefer not to apply the word *evolution* to the changes within kinds, that does not involve spontaneous generation of new genetic information. We prefer to use the term *speciation* for this concept, as it is more scientifically rigorous to narrow the definition of biological evolution. But the bait-and-switch approach of evolutionists deliberately confuses speciation with molecules-to-man evolution.

Evolution and Information Theory

This concept of information in evolution, as a scientific concept, has been described in detail by Dr Werner Gitt, in his book *In the Beginning Was Information*. Gitt argues that there are five levels of information, namely:

1. Statistics
2. Syntax
3. Semantics
4. Pragmatics
5. Apobetics[1]

Gitt gives a full discussion of the definitions of these levels in chapter 4 of his book. A brief summary is provided here.

Statistical information is carried simply by the number of occurrences of letters and words. My word cloud was an example of statistical information. Many evolutionists have assumed that genetic information could arise by statistics alone. This is the idea that gave rise to the mythology that an infinite number of monkeys with typewriters could reproduce the works of Shakespeare.

Syntax refers to the fact that only certain combinations of letters and symbols have meaning. For example, we expect "cat" to mean something, but "xcy" does not - at least in English. In one lecture for children, Richard Dawkins got children to draw out a Scrabble letter at random from a bag. Eventually, three children drew out the letters c, a and t in order. Dawkins declared that this was the beginning of information. It is not. Dr. Gitt himself

would not have been brought up thinking that *cat* is a word, because he is German! In other words, the decoding of such "random" information is only possible with the pre-existence of the language skills required.

The third level is **semantics**. At this level, we try to determine what was in the mind of the sender, because this might make a difference to the message. If you read a text that says "Are you back home already?", you have no idea whether the sender is happy or irritated by the possibility of the answer "yes". On the other hand, the tone of voice of the questioner might hold more information on that subject. The semantic level of information has led to famous quibbles over the exact use of words. One of the more famous examples of this was during the impeachment hearings in 1998. Questioned about his previous statements about his relationship with Monica Lewinsky, President Bill Clinton responded thus:

> *Challenged later in the hearing, he argued the meaning of the smallest of words contained in one of his lawyers' statements.*

> *"It depends upon what the meaning of the word 'is' is. If 'is' means 'is and never has been' that's one thing - if it means*

---

[1] Gitt, W. (2005), *In the Beginning Was Information*, (Green Forest, AR: Master Books), pp58-82

'there is none', that was a completely true statement," he said.[1]

Another politician also, famously, got into difficulties over the precise meaning of simple words, though in the case of Donald Rumsfeld, who was much scorned at the time, there are many people today who say that his clarification on language was actually very accurate and very clear.

Reports that say that something hasn't happened are always interesting to me, because as we know, there are known knowns; there are things we know we know. We also know there are known unknowns; that is to say we know there are some things we do not know. But there are also unknown unknowns -- the ones we don't know we don't know. And if one looks

throughout the history of our country and other free countries, it is the latter category that tend to be the difficult ones.[2]

Pragmatics is the the fourth level, and this level acknowledges that information is only information if it leads to actions.

[2]
< http://www.defense.gov/transcripts/transcript.aspx ?transcriptid=2636 >

Illustration of Humpty Dumpty from Through the Looking Glass, by John Tenniel, 1871. Public Domain (copyright expired)

[1]
< http://news.bbc.co.uk/o nthisday/hi/dates/stories /september/21/newsid_25 25000/2525339.stm >, retrieved July 5th 2015

Finally, **apobetics** establishes a required purpose for the information, and tests to see if that purpose is fulfilled.

It is Gitt's contention that the information carried by DNA fulfils all five levels of information science, whereas many evolutionists restrict the information to only the lowest level. Logic, as well as experience, suggests that Gitt is right.

There's Glory for You

The arguments that this book is concentrating on are specifically to do with language, its use and its misuse. So it seems that a fun place to end this chapter would be to look at how the meaning of words was mangled by Humpty Dumpty in Lewis Carroll's second book about Alice Liddle - *Through the Looking Glass.* It has been established as the norm in the Alice books that this little girl speaks with more maturity and common sense than the adult characters around her. In this scene, Humpty Dumpty has been explaining to her the concept of un-birthdays, and how they are much better than birthdays, because you only have one birthday a year, whereas you will have 364 un-birthdays every year. To round off the culmination of his argument on the subject, Humpty Dumpty exclaims:

'There's glory for you!'

'I don't know what you mean by "glory,"' Alice said.

Humpty Dumpty smiled contemptuously. 'Of course you don't—till I tell you. I meant "there's a nice knock-down argument for you!"'

It sometimes seems trivial to comment on children's literature like this - rather like having to explain a joke - but Carroll included passages such as this for a reason, and his audience was really an adult audience. So the Great Egg has defied normal laws of conversation. He should be using words that the other person understands. Instead, he uses a word that Alice does not understand in this new context. Humpty then argues that *glory* means "there's a nice knock-down argument for you!" Of course, glory does not mean this, as sensible Alice goes on to explain. If Humpty Dumpty gets away with this change in meaning, then no one will be sure what is meant when the word is used in its original meaning. This is precisely the problem so often with the use of the word *evolution*, and explains why such words should be carefully defined.

'But "glory" doesn't mean "a nice knock-down argument,"' Alice objected.

'When I use a word,' Humpty Dumpty said in rather a scornful tone, 'it means

just what I choose it to mean—neither more nor less.'

'The question is,' said Alice, 'whether you CAN make words mean so many different things.'

'The question is,' said Humpty Dumpty, 'which is to be master—that's all.'[1]

[1] Carroll, L. (1871), *Through the Looking Glass, and What Alice Found there*, (Millennium Fulcrum Edition 1.7, Kindle - public domain), locations 660-670

To twist our quotations together, Humpty Dumpty may be mad, but there is method in't. And his madness has proved infectious, because his scornful, "adult" put-downs to Alice are analogous to the same arrogance shown to the public by so many evolutionary scientists.

Chapter 6

FUZZY WORD ANALYSIS

At long last, we get to the practical element of this book. In the preceding chapters, I have given you justification for our methodology (chapters 1 and 5), and definitions for the three types of evolutionary language that we are going to search for (chapters 2, 3 and 4). Now I am going to show you how to put the ideas into practice, with a very simple technique. I have been using this technique for some time with audiences at my talks, and, initially, I was concentrating only on fuzzy words. So I called the technique *Fuzzy Word Analysis.* The technique has now been extended to take in magic words and words of worldview bias. However, audiences have got used to *fuzzy word analysis* (or FWA), so I am going to stick with that term, even if I am using magic or worldview words.

Materials

You need four colors of highlighters. Any four colors will do, but you had better make yourself a key, and stick to the same 4 colors, in order to avoid confusion. The four colors are going to be for 1. Fuzzy

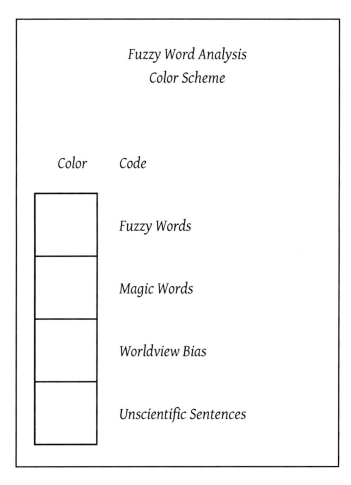

Fuzzy Word Analysis
Color Scheme

Color   Code

Fuzzy Words

Magic Words

Worldview Bias

Unscientific Sentences

Words, 2. Magic Words, 3. Worldview Bias, and 4. Unscientific sentences. I have already introduced you to the first 3 - I will explain the 4th item when we get to it.

For your purposes, I suggest you color in the boxes in the key provided on this page, so that you remember what your color scheme is. You will also find this scheme repeated.

My personal color scheme is: 1. Fuzzy Words (Yellow), 2. Magic Words (Pink), 3. Worldview Bias (Blue), 4. Unscientific sentences (Gray - I usually use graphite pencil).

FWA Summary

The technique can be explained quickly, so that it is easy to remember.

1. Work through your science article, highlighting all the fuzzy words.

2. Go through again, and highlight all the magic words.

3. On your third pass through the article, highlight the words of worldview bias.

4. Finally, mark off all the sentences that contain any of the first three highlightings.

5. Anything left unhighlighted in the article is real science. You will be surprised how little real science there is in each article.

Human Brain Gene

In order to follow the technique better, we really need to examine a few case studies.

Consider the article on the next page, entitled "Gene which sparked human brain leap identified".

As in the summary, our first task is to find the fuzzy words. So the article is reproduced on the following page, with the fuzzy words identified. The page after that explains the reason for the fuzzy word highlighting.

I have used the key below for my fuzzy word analysis.

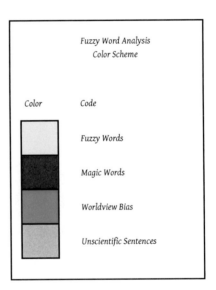

Sample Science Article

Gene which sparked human brain leap identified

Scientists have identified the gene which may have driven the crucial step in evolution where man learned to talk.

Nick Collins, Science Correspondent, Date: 3 May 2012 Time: 07:38 PM BST

<‹http://www.telegraph.co.uk/science/evolution/9244310/Gene-which-sparked-human-brain-leap-identified.html›

Although humans and chimpanzees separated six million years ago, we still share 96 per cent of our genome and the gene is one of only about 30 which have copied themselves since that time

By duplicating itself two and a half million years ago the gene could have given early human brains the power of speech and invention, leaving cousins such as chimpanzees behind.

The gene, known as SRGAP2, helps control the development of the neocortex – the part of the brain responsible for higher functions like language and conscious thought.

Having an extra copies slowed down the development of the brain, allowing it to forge more connections between nerve cells and in doing so grow bigger and more complex, researchers said.

In a study published in the Cell journal, the scientists reported that the gene duplicated about 3.5 million years ago to create a "daughter" gene, and again a million years later creating a "granddaughter" copy.

Although humans and chimpanzees separated six million years ago, we still share 96 per cent of our genome and the gene is one of only about 30 which have copied themselves since that time.

The first duplication was relatively inactive but the second occurred at about the time when primitive Homo separated from its brother Australopithecus species and began developing more sophisticated tools and behaviours.

Evan Eichler at the University of Washington, who led the research, said the benefit of the duplication would have been instant, meaning human ancestors could have distanced themselves from rival species within a generation.

He said: "This innovation could not have happened without that incomplete duplication. Our data suggest a mechanism where incomplete duplication of this gene created a novel function 'at birth'."

Information taken from the Daily Telegraph, and used under 'fair use' for educational purposes.

Sample Science Article

Gene which sparked human brain leap identified

Scientists have identified the gene which may have driven the crucial step in evolution where man learned to talk.

Nick Collins, Science Correspondent, Date: 3 May 2012 Time: 07:38 PM BST

<‹http://www.telegraph.co.uk/science/evolution/9244310/Gene-which-sparked-human-brain-leap-identified.html›>

Although humans and chimpanzees separated six million years ago, we still share 96 per cent of our genome and the gene is one of only about 30 which have copied themselves since that time

By duplicating itself two and a half million years ago the gene could have given early human brains the power of speech and invention, leaving cousins such as chimpanzees behind.

The gene, known as SRGAP2, helps control the development of the neocortex – the part of the brain responsible for higher functions like language and conscious thought.

Having an extra copies slowed down the development of the brain, allowing it to forge more connections between nerve cells and in doing so grow bigger and more complex, researchers said.

In a study published in the Cell journal, the scientists reported that the gene duplicated about 3.5 million

years ago to create a "daughter" gene, and again a million years later creating a "granddaughter" copy.

Although humans and chimpanzees separated six million years ago, we still share 96 per cent of our genome and the gene is one of only about 30 which have copied themselves since that time.

The first duplication was relatively inactive but the second occurred at about the time when primitive Homo separated from its brother Australopithecus species and began developing more sophisticated tools and behaviours.

Evan Eichler at the University of Washington, who led the research, said the benefit of the duplication would have been instant, meaning human ancestors could have distanced themselves from rival species within a generation.

He said: "This innovation could not have happened without that incomplete duplication. Our data suggest a mechanism where incomplete duplication of this gene created a novel function 'at birth'."

Information taken from the Daily Telegraph, and used under 'fair use' for educational purposes.

Marking Up the Fuzzy Words

Note:
All the worksheets used here have been taken from public websites. The amount of information used is minimal, and is allowed under "fair use", as comment and criticism is being made of the content. Web addresses where the content can be viewed complete and unaltered are given on each sheet.

Most fuzzy words on this page are of the type "may have, would have" etc

Using reported speech, such as "researchers said" or "scientists reported" is often a way of deflecting responsibility from certain comments.

On the next page, you will see the worksheet with all the magic words marked up. All the magic words on this sheet are to do with millions of years. The pages after that show the mark-up of words of Worldview Bias, followed by an explanation of each.

Gene which sparked human brain leap identified

Scientists have identified the gene which may have driven the crucial step in evolution where man learned to talk.

Nick Collins, Science Correspondent, Date: 3 May 2012 Time: 07:38 PM BST

<http://www.telegraph.co.uk/science/evolution/9244310/Gene-which-sparked-human-brain-leap-identified.html>

Although humans and chimpanzees separated six million years ago, we still share 96 per cent of our genome and the gene is one of only about 30 which have copied themselves since that time

By duplicating itself two and a half million years ago the gene could have given early human brains the power of speech and invention, leaving cousins such as chimpanzees behind.

The gene, known as SRGAP2, helps control the development of the neocortex – the part of the brain responsible for higher functions like language and conscious thought.

Having an extra copies slowed down the development of the brain, allowing it to forge more connections between nerve cells and in doing so grow bigger and more complex, researchers said.

In a study published in the Cell journal, the scientists reported that the gene duplicated about 3.5 million

years ago to create a "daughter" gene, and again a million years later creating a "granddaughter" copy.

Although humans and chimpanzees separated six million years ago, we still share 96 per cent of our genome and the gene is one of only about 30 which have copied themselves since that time.

The first duplication was relatively inactive but the second occurred at about the time when primitive Homo separated from its brother Australopithecus species and began developing more sophisticated tools and behaviours.

Evan Eichler at the University of Washington, who led the research, said the benefit of the duplication would have been instant, meaning human ancestors could have distanced themselves from rival species within a generation.

He said: "This innovation could not have happened without that incomplete duplication. Our data suggest a mechanism where incomplete duplication of this gene created a novel function 'at birth'."

Information taken from the Daily Telegraph, and used under 'fair use' for educational purposes.

Sample Science Article

Gene which sparked human brain leap identified

Scientists have identified the gene which may have driven the crucial step in evolution where man learned to talk.

Nick Collins, Science Correspondent, Date: 3 May 2012 Time: 07:38 PM BST

<http://www.telegraph.co.uk/science/evolution/9244310/Gene-which-sparked-human-brain-leap-identified.html>

years ago to create a "daughter" gene, and again a million years later creating a "granddaughter" copy.

Although humans and chimpanzees separated six million years ago, we still share 96 per cent of our genome and the gene is one of only about 30 which have copied themselves since that time.

Although humans and chimpanzees separated six million years ago, we still share 96 per cent of our genome and the gene is one of only about 30 which have copied themselves since that time

By duplicating itself two and a half million years ago the gene could have given early human brains the power of speech and invention, leaving cousins such as chimpanzees behind.

The gene, known as SRGAP2, helps control the development of the neocortex – the part of the brain responsible for higher functions like language and conscious thought.

Having an extra copies slowed down the development of the brain, allowing it to forge more connections between nerve cells and in doing so grow bigger and more complex, researchers said.

In a study published in the Cell journal, the scientists reported that the gene duplicated about 3.5 million

The first duplication was relatively inactive but the second occurred at about the time when primitive Homo separated from its brother Australopithecus species and began developing more sophisticated tools and behaviours.

Evan Eichler at the University of Washington, who led the research, said the benefit of the duplication would have been instant, meaning human ancestors could have distanced themselves from rival species within a generation.

He said: "This innovation could not have happened without that incomplete duplication. Our data suggest a mechanism where incomplete duplication of this gene created a novel function 'at birth'."

Information taken from the Daily Telegraph, and used under 'fair use' for educational purposes.

Sample Science Article

Gene which sparked human brain

leap identified

Scientists have identified the gene which may have driven the crucial step in evolution where man learned to talk.

Nick Collins, Science Correspondent, Date: 3 May 2012 Time: 07:38 PM BST

Although humans and chimpanzees separated six million years ago, we still share 96 per cent of our genome and the gene is one of only about 30 which have copied themselves since that time

By duplicating itself two and a half million years ago the gene could have given early human brains the power of speech and invention, leaving cousins such as chimpanzees behind.

The gene, known as SRGAP2, helps control the development of the neocortex – the part of the brain responsible for higher functions like language and conscious thought.

Having an extra copies slowed down the development of the brain, allowing it to forge more connections between nerve cells and in doing so grow bigger and more complex, researchers said.

In a study published in the Cell journal, the scientists reported that the gene duplicated about 3.5 million

years ago to create a "daughter" gene, and again a million years later creating a "granddaughter" copy.

Although humans and chimpanzees separated six million years ago, we still share 96 per cent of our genome and the gene is one of only about 30 which have copied themselves since that time.

The first duplication was relatively inactive but the second occurred at about the time when primitive Homo separated from its brother Australopithecus species and began developing more sophisticated tools and behaviours.

Evan Eichler at the University of Washington, who led the research, said the benefit of the duplication would have been instant, meaning human ancestors could have distanced themselves from rival species within a generation.

He said: "This innovation could not have happened without that incomplete duplication. Our data suggest a mechanism where incomplete duplication of this gene created a novel function 'at birth'."

Information taken from the Daily Telegraph, and used under 'fair use' for educational purposes.

Words of Worldview Bias

"Sparked" implies something happening spontaneously.

This 96% is only a percentage of that DNA that has been preselected for evolutionary reasons. Therefore thus is not a far test

"Cousins" is an emotive word, and, we think, unjustifiable in this case.

Gene which sparked human brain leap identified

Scientists have identified the gene which may have driven the crucial step in evolution where man learned to talk.

Nick Collins, Science Correspondent, Date: 3 May 2012 Time: 07:38 PM BST

Although humans and chimpanzees separated six million years ago, we still share 96 per cent of our genome and the gene is one of only about 30 which have copied themselves since that time

By duplicating itself two and a half million years ago the gene could have given early human brains the power of speech and invention, leaving cousins such as chimpanzees behind.

The gene, known as SRGAP2, helps control the development of the neocortex – the part of the brain responsible for higher functions like language and conscious thought.

Having an extra copies slowed down the development of the brain, allowing it to forge more connections between nerve cells and in doing so grow bigger and more complex, researchers said.

In a study published in the Cell journal, the scientists reported that the gene duplicated about 3.5 million

years ago to create a "daughter" gene, and again a million years later creating a "granddaughter" copy.

Although humans and chimpanzees separated six million years ago, we still share 96 per cent of our genome and the gene is one of only about 30 which have copied themselves since that time.

The first duplication was relatively inactive but the second occurred at about the time when primitive Homo separated from its brother Australopithecus species and began developing more sophisticated tools and behaviours.

Evan Eichler at the University of Washington, who led the research, said the benefit of the duplication would have been instant, meaning human ancestors could have distanced themselves from rival species within a generation.

He said: "This innovation could not have happened without that incomplete duplication. Our data suggest a mechanism where incomplete duplication of this gene created a novel function 'at birth'."

Information taken from the Daily Telegraph, and used under 'fair use' for educational purposes.

"Brother" is also an unjustified word

Innovation is really a term of personation, or reification. There is no personality that can innovate

Since no real experiment has been done, it is not possible for the scientists to estimate anything about rates, let alone discuss how the rate has decelerated

In the last stage overleaf, we use gray (pencil) to go over any sentence that contains any of the 3 types of words that we are analyzing. The only real science in this article is that left with a white background.

Sample Science Article

Gene which sparked human brain

leap identified

Scientists have identified the gene which may have driven the crucial step in evolution where man learned to talk.

Nick Collins, Science Correspondent, Date: 3 May 2012 Time: 07:38 PM BST

Although humans and chimpanzees separated six million years ago, we still share 96 per cent of our genome and the gene is one of only about 30 which have copied themselves since that time

By duplicating itself two and a half million years ago the gene could have given early human brains the power of speech and invention, leaving cousins such as chimpanzees behind.

The gene, known as SRGAP2, helps control the development of the neocortex – the part of the brain responsible for higher functions like language and conscious thought.

Having an extra copies slowed down the development of the brain, allowing it to forge more connections between nerve cells and in doing so grow bigger and more complex, researchers said.

In a study published in the Cell journal, the scientists reported that the gene duplicated about 3.5 million

years ago to create a "daughter" gene, and again a million years later creating a "granddaughter" copy.

Although humans and chimpanzees separated six million years ago, we still share 96 per cent of our genome and the gene is one of only about 30 which have copied themselves since that time.

The first duplication was relatively inactive but the second occurred at about the time when primitive Homo separated from its brother Australopithecus species and began developing more sophisticated tools and behaviours.

Evan Eichler at the University of Washington, who led the research, said the benefit of the duplication would have been instant, meaning human ancestors could have distanced themselves from rival species within a generation.

He said: "This innovation could not have happened without that incomplete duplication. Our data suggest a mechanism where incomplete duplication of this gene created a novel function 'at birth'."

Information taken from the Daily Telegraph, and used under 'fair use' for educational purposes.

Ancient Fig Wasp

We will take a little more time over this article about the Ancient Fig Wasp, though the technique is still the same. Remember that the marking-up will be:

1. Fuzzy Words

2. Magic Words

3. Words of Worldview Bias

4. Unscientific Sentences

Look carefully a the Fig Wasp article on the next page, then at the marking up for fuzzy words.

Fuzzy Words

1. The phrase "researchers say" is being used to qualify an unscientific conjecture.

2. "It's possible" is also introducing a conjecture.

3. "Not hard evidence" is a tacit admission of speculation

4. "It is possible" - as above

5. "Indicate" - no details are given abou the "current studies", so the word indicate is merely being used to deflect possible criticism

6. "Could be an example of" and "could be the ancestor of" are phrases introducing concepts in an unwarranted manner.

7. "Offers new insights" - this is a common reconstruction, when an observation that obviously does not fit in with current theory shows up.

Magic Words

All examples shown are indicative of the impossible becoming "possible", given millions of years.

Words of Worldview Bias

There are some fascinating phrases of bias.

Cretaceous Research.. Is this research done in the Cretaceous period, or research about it? An evolutionist would aay that it must be research about the Cretaceous, but, in a Baconian scientific sense, this is just as impossible as conducting research IN the Cretaceous.

First Occurrence. This is a presuppositional conjecture, as there is no evidence of timescale available.

Convergent Evolution.. This is the concept that two different species have evolved in similar ways independently. This is also a conjecture, without hard evidence. Simply stating that this "could be an example" is not helpful scientifically.

Sample Science Article

Ancient 'Fig Wasp' Lived Tens of Millions of Years

Before Figs

PUBLISHED: December 5th 2013 Read more: http://www.sciencedaily.com/releases/2013/12/131205141625.htm

A 115-million-year-old fossilized wasp from northeast Brazil presents a baffling puzzle to researchers. The wasp's ovipositor, the organ through which it lays its eggs, looks a lot like those of present-day wasps that lay their eggs in figs. The problem, researchers say, is that figs arose about 65 million years after this wasp was alive.

A report of the findings appears in the journal Cretaceous Research.

The wasp belongs to the Hymenoptera superfamily known as Chalcidoidea, which parasitize other insects, spiders and some plants. The group includes about 22,000 known species and is estimated to contain up to 500,000 species.

"This is a tiny parasitic wasp, it's the smallest fossil wasp found in this particular deposit and it's the oldest representative of its family," said Sam Heads, a paleoentomologist at the Illinois Natural History Survey at the University of Illinois. "More importantly, it's possible that this wasp was fig-associated, which is interesting because it's Early Cretaceous, about 115 to 120 million years old. That's a good 65 million years or so prior to the first occurrence of figs in the fossil record."

Heads worked in collaboration with University of Portsmouth scientists Nathan Barling and David Martill.

The new findings demonstrate the value of studying insect fossils, Heads said.

"The fossil record of insects is very extensive both geographically and temporally. It goes back 415 to 420 million years and preserves the ancestral forms of a lot of the insects that are alive today," he said. "So it's a great resource for understanding insect evolutionary history and the distribution of insects across the planet in the past."

The presence of a wasp with an ovipositor that looks like those used by fig wasps today is not hard evidence that figs were around in the fossil wasp's day -- a time of dinosaurs, Heads said.

"There is no evidence of the existence of figs at this time and the most recent molecular study doesn't place figs that far back," he said. While it is possible that figs are

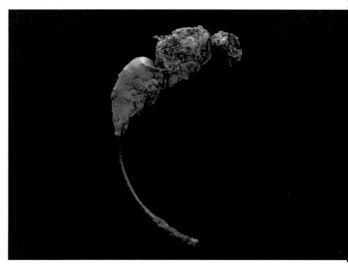

Although it lived roughly 65 million years before the earliest known occurrence of figs, the fossil wasp's ovipositor closely resembles those of today's fig wasps. (Credit: Nathan Barling and Sam Heads)

older than current studies indicate, it is also possible that "something like a fig was around and this wasp was parasitizing whatever that was."

This could be an example of convergent evolution, where separate species independently evolve similar traits, he said. Or the fossil wasp could be the ancestor of the fig wasp, and its ovipositor, first adapted to a plant or fruit that was around long before the fig, later found a use in figs.

Comparing insect fossils with living organisms offers new insights into the natural history of insects, the plants they pollinate and their hosts or prey, Heads said. This differs significantly from studies of the fossils of animals that have become extinct.

"When you talk about paleontology to people the first thing they think of is dinosaurs," he said. "And that's great. Dinosaurs are really exciting, wonderful animals. But for the most part, they're extinct. With insects and other arthropods like spiders and scorpions, they're around still. So we have modern forms to compare our fossil forms to, which is incredibly useful."

Ancient 'Fig Wasp' Lived Tens of Millions of Years Before Figs

Sample FWA Worksheet

PUBLISHED: December 5th 2013 Read more: http://www.sciencedaily.com/releases/2013/12/131205141625.htm

1. A 115-million-year-old fossilized wasp from northeast Brazil presents a baffling puzzle to researchers. The wasp's ovipositor, the organ through which it lays its eggs, looks a lot like those of present-day wasps that lay their eggs in figs. The problem, researchers say, is that figs arose about 65 million years after this wasp was alive.

A report of the findings appears in the journal Cretaceous Research.

The wasp belongs to the Hymenoptera superfamily known as Chalcidoidea, which parasitize other insects, spiders and some plants. The group includes about 22,000 known species and is estimated to contain up to 500,000 species.

"This is a tiny parasitic wasp, it's the smallest fossil wasp found in this particular deposit and it's the oldest representative of its family," said Sam Heads, a paleoentomologist at the Illinois Natural History Survey at

2. the University of Illinois. "More importantly, it's possible that this wasp was fig-associated, which is interesting because it's Early Cretaceous, about 115 to 120 million years old. That's a good 65 million years or so prior to the first occurrence of figs in the fossil record."

Heads worked in collaboration with University of Portsmouth scientists Nathan Barling and David Martill.

3. The new findings demonstrate the value of studying insect fossils, Heads said.

"The fossil record of insects is very extensive both geographically and temporally. It goes back 415 to 420 million years and preserves the ancestral forms of a lot of the insects that are alive today," he said. "So it's a great resource for understanding insect evolutionary history and the distribution of insects across the planet in the past."

4. The presence of a wasp with an ovipositor that looks like those used by fig wasps today is not hard evidence that figs were around in the fossil wasp's day -- a time of dinosaurs, Heads said.

"There is no evidence of the existence of figs at this time and the most recent molecular study doesn't place figs that far back," he said. While it is possible that figs are older than current studies indicate, it is also possible that

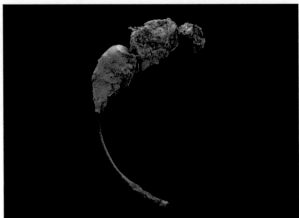

Although it lived roughly 65 million years before the earliest known occurrence of figs, the fossil wasp's ovipositor closely resembles those of today's fig wasps. (Credit: Nathan Barling and Sam Heads)

"something like a fig was around and this wasp was parasitizing whatever that was."

This could be an example of convergent evolution, where separate species independently evolve similar traits, he said. Or the fossil wasp could be the ancestor of the fig wasp, and its ovipositor, first adapted to a plant or fruit that was around long before the fig, later found a use in figs.

Comparing insect fossils with living organisms offers new insights into the natural history of insects, the plants they pollinate and their hosts or prey, Heads said. This differs significantly from studies of the fossils of animals that have become extinct.

"When you talk about paleontology to people the first thing they think of is dinosaurs," he said. "And that's great. Dinosaurs are really exciting, wonderful animals. But for the most part, they're extinct. With insects and other arthropods like spiders and scorpions, they're around still. So we have modern forms to compare our fossil forms to, which is incredibly useful."

5.

6.

7.

Sample Science Article

Ancient 'Fig Wasp' Lived Tens of Millions of Years Before Figs

PUBLISHED: December 5th 2013 Read more: http://www.sciencedaily.com/releases/2013/12/131205141625.htm

A 115-million-year-old fossilized wasp from northeast Brazil presents a baffling puzzle to researchers. The wasp's ovipositor, the organ through which it lays its eggs, looks a lot like those of present-day wasps that lay their eggs in figs. The problem, researchers say, is that figs arose about 65 million years after this wasp was alive.

A report of the findings appears in the journal Cretaceous Research.

The wasp belongs to the Hymenoptera superfamily known as Chalcidoidea, which parasitize other insects, spiders and some plants. The group includes about 22,000 known species and is estimated to contain up to 500,000 species.

"This is a tiny parasitic wasp, it's the smallest fossil wasp found in this particular deposit and it's the oldest representative of its family," said Sam Heads, a paleoentomologist at the Illinois Natural History Survey at the University of Illinois. "More importantly, it's possible that this wasp was fig-associated, which is interesting because it's Early Cretaceous, about 115 to 120 million years old. That's a good 65 million years or so prior to the first occurrence of figs in the fossil record."

Heads worked in collaboration with University of Portsmouth scientists Nathan Barling and David Martill.

The new findings demonstrate the value of studying insect fossils, Heads said.

"The fossil record of insects is very extensive both geographically and temporally. It goes back 415 to 420 million years and preserves the ancestral forms of a lot of the insects that are alive today," he said. "So it's a great resource for understanding insect evolutionary history and the distribution of insects across the planet in the past."

The presence of a wasp with an ovipositor that looks like those used by fig wasps today is not hard evidence that figs were around in the fossil wasp's day -- a time of dinosaurs, Heads said.

"There is no evidence of the existence of figs at this time and the most recent molecular study doesn't place figs that far back," he said. While it is possible that figs are

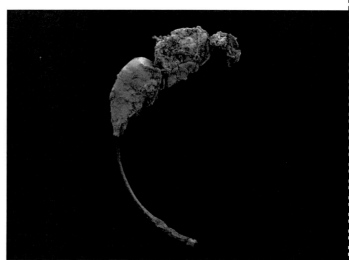

Although it lived roughly 65 million years before the earliest known occurrence of figs, the fossil wasp's ovipositor closely resembles those of today's fig wasps. (Credit: Nathan Barling and Sam Heads)

older than current studies indicate, it is also possible that "something like a fig was around and this wasp was parasitizing whatever that was."

This could be an example of convergent evolution, where separate species independently evolve similar traits, he said. Or the fossil wasp could be the ancestor of the fig wasp, and its ovipositor, first adapted to a plant or fruit that was around long before the fig, later found a use in figs.

Comparing insect fossils with living organisms offers new insights into the natural history of insects, the plants they pollinate and their hosts or prey, Heads said. This differs significantly from studies of the fossils of animals that have become extinct.

"When you talk about paleontology to people the first thing they think of is dinosaurs," he said. "And that's great. Dinosaurs are really exciting, wonderful animals. But for the most part, they're extinct. With insects and other arthropods like spiders and scorpions, they're around still. So we have modern forms to compare our fossil forms to, which is incredibly useful."

Ancient 'Fig Wasp' Lived Tens of Millions of Years Before Figs

PUBLISHED: December 5th 2013 Read more: http://www.sciencedaily.com/releases/2013/12/131205141625.htm

A 115-million-year-old fossilized wasp from northeast Brazil presents a baffling puzzle to researchers. The wasp's ovipositor, the organ through which it lays its eggs, looks a lot like those of present-day wasps that lay their eggs in figs. The problem, researchers say, is that figs arose about 65 million years after this wasp was alive.

A report of the findings appears in the journal Cretaceous Research.

The wasp belongs to the Hymenoptera superfamily known as Chalcidoidea, which parasitize other insects, spiders and some plants. The group includes about 22,000 known species and is estimated to contain up to 500,000 species.

"This is a tiny parasitic wasp, it's the smallest fossil wasp found in this particular deposit and it's the oldest representative of its family," said Sam Heads, a paleoentomologist at the Illinois Natural History Survey at the University of Illinois. "More importantly, it's possible that this wasp was fig-associated, which is interesting because it's Early Cretaceous, about 115 to 120 million years old. That's a good 65 million years or so prior to the first occurrence of figs in the fossil record."

Heads worked in collaboration with University of Portsmouth scientists Nathan Barling and David Martill.

The new findings demonstrate the value of studying insect fossils, Heads said.

"The fossil record of insects is very extensive both geographically and temporally. It goes back 415 to 420 million years and preserves the ancestral forms of a lot of the insects that are alive today," he said. "So it's a great resource for understanding insect evolutionary history and the distribution of insects across the planet in the past."

The presence of a wasp with an ovipositor that looks like those used by fig wasps today is not hard evidence that figs were around in the fossil wasp's day -- a time of dinosaurs, Heads said.

"There is no evidence of the existence of figs at this time and the most recent molecular study doesn't place figs that far back," he said. While it is possible that figs are

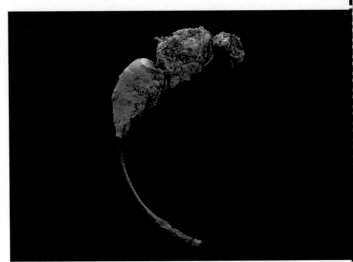

Although it lived roughly 65 million years before the earliest known occurrence of figs, the fossil wasp's ovipositor closely resembles those of today's fig wasps. (Credit: Nathan Barling and Sam Heads)

older than current studies indicate, it is also possible that "something like a fig was around and this wasp was parasitizing whatever that was."

This could be an example of convergent evolution, where separate species independently evolve similar traits, he said. Or the fossil wasp could be the ancestor of the fig wasp, and its ovipositor, first adapted to a plant or fruit that was around long before the fig, later found a use in figs.

Comparing insect fossils with living organisms offers new insights into the natural history of insects, the plants they pollinate and their hosts or prey, Heads said. This differs significantly from studies of the fossils of animals that have become extinct.

"When you talk about paleontology to people the first thing they think of is dinosaurs," he said. "And that's great! Dinosaurs are really exciting, wonderful animals. But for the most part, they're extinct. With insects and other arthropods like spiders and scorpions, they're around still. So we have modern forms to compare our fossil forms to, which is incredibly useful."

Sample Science Article

Ancient 'Fig Wasp' Lived Tens of Millions of Years Before Figs

Sample FWA Worksheet

PUBLISHED: December 5th 2013 Read more: http://www.sciencedaily.com/releases/2013/12/131205141625.htm

A 115-million-year-old fossilized wasp from northeast Brazil presents a baffling puzzle to researchers. The wasp's ovipositor, the organ through which it lays its eggs, looks a lot like those of present-day wasps that lay their eggs in figs. The problem, researchers say, is that figs arose about 65 million years after this wasp was alive.

A report of the findings appears in the journal Cretaceous Research.

The wasp belongs to the Hymenoptera superfamily known as Chalcidoidea, which parasitize other insects, spiders and some plants. The group includes about 22,000 known species and is estimated to contain up to 500,000 species.

"This is a tiny parasitic wasp, it's the smallest fossil wasp found in this particular deposit and it's the oldest representative of its family," said Sam Heads, a paleoentomologist at the Illinois Natural History Survey at the University of Illinois. "More importantly, it's possible that this wasp was fig-associated, which is interesting because it's Early Cretaceous, about 115 to 120 million years old. That's a good 65 million years or so prior to the first occurrence of figs in the fossil record."

Heads worked in collaboration with University of Portsmouth scientists Nathan Barling and David Martill.

The new findings demonstrate the value of studying insect fossils, Heads said.

"The fossil record of insects is very extensive both geographically and temporally. It goes back 415 to 420 million years and preserves the ancestral forms of a lot of the insects that are alive today," he said. "So it's a great resource for understanding insect evolutionary history and the distribution of insects across the planet in the past."

The presence of a wasp with an ovipositor that looks like those used by fig wasps today is not hard evidence that figs were around in the fossil wasp's day -- a time of dinosaurs, Heads said.

"There is no evidence of the existence of figs at this time and the most recent molecular study doesn't place figs that far back," he said. While it is possible that figs are

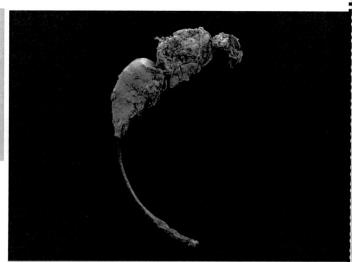

Although it lived roughly 65 million years before the earliest known occurrence of figs, the fossil wasp's ovipositor closely resembles those of today's fig wasps. (Credit: Nathan Barling and Sam Heads)

older than current studies indicate, it is also possible that "something like a fig was around and this wasp was parasitizing whatever that was."

This could be an example of convergent evolution, where separate species independently evolve similar traits, he said. Or the fossil wasp could be the ancestor of the fig wasp, and its ovipositor, first adapted to a plant or fruit that was around long before the fig, later found a use in figs.

Comparing insect fossils with living organisms offers new insights into the natural history of insects, the plants they pollinate and their hosts or prey, Heads said. This differs significantly from studies of the fossils of animals that have become extinct.

"When you talk about paleontology to people the first thing they think of is dinosaurs," he said. "And that's great. Dinosaurs are really exciting, wonderful animals. But for the most part, they're extinct. With insects and other arthropods like spiders and scorpions, they're around still. So we have modern forms to compare our fossil forms to, which is incredibly useful."

Astronomers Witness a Star Being Born

One of the oldest chestnuts in long-age propaganda is the idea that we can witness a star being born. This article from Yale University (on the next page) talks about this phenomenon. In fact, no one is witnessing a star being born - a process which is supposed to take millions of years. They are definitely seeing something significant, but the idea that their observation is a snapshot of the birth of a star is made only because the evidence is being deliberately interpreted that way.

The first paragraph has examples of all three of our types of analysis.

Fuzzy Words: The phrase "could be" indicates that this is a conjecture, rather than a statement of science.

Magic Words: Magic words often refer to millions of years. But we have already discussed how gravity can be used to invoke evolutionary magic. The impossible accretion of material into a new star is supposedly accomplished by the magic of gravity, but there is no possible mechanism for this to happen.

> Astronomers have glimpsed what could be the youngest known star at the very moment it is being born. Not yet fully developed into a true star, the object is in the earliest stages of star formation and has just begun pulling in matter from a surrounding envelope of gas and dust, according to a new study that appears in the current issue of the Astrophysical Journal.

Words of Worldview Bias: Finally, we see a number of words that have no scientific basis, other than the bias of the writer. The image is offered as an example of the "youngest" type of star,, without justifying how the star could be "young". The star is said to be "at the very moment it is being born", and "not fully developed" and in "the earliest stages". None of these phrases prove anything. They are merely indicative of the worldview which the author s using to interpret what is being seen. These interpretations are unjustified.

Having looked at this paragraph, try to complete the highlighting for the rest of the article.

Some more worksheets for you to practice on can be found in the Appendix. I suggest that you photocopy these, and use the highlighter on the copied version.

Sample Science Article

Astronomers Witness a Star Being Born

PUBLISHED: June 17 2010

Read more: http://news.yale.edu/2010/06/17/astronomers-witness-star-being-born

Astronomers have glimpsed what could be the youngest known star at the very moment it is being born. Not yet fully developed into a true star, the object is in the earliest stages of star formation and has just begun pulling in matter from a surrounding envelope of gas and dust, according to a new study that appears in the current issue of the Astrophysical Journal.

The study's authors—who include astronomers from Yale University, the Harvard-Smithsonian Center for Astrophysics and the Max Planck Institute for Astronomy in Germany—found the object using the Submillimeter Array in Hawaii and the Spitzer Space Telescope. Known as L1448-IRS2E, it's located in the Perseus star-forming region, about 800 light years away within our Milky Way galaxy.

Astronomers caught a glimpse of a future star just as it is being born out of the surrounding gas and dust, in a star-forming region similar to the one pictured above. (Photo: NASA, ESA)

Stars form out of large, cold, dense regions of gas and dust called molecular clouds, which exist throughout the galaxy. Astronomers think L1448-IRS2E is in between the prestellar phase, when a particularly dense region of a molecular cloud first begins to clump together, and the protostar phase, when gravity has pulled enough material together to form a dense, hot core out of the surrounding envelope.

"It's very difficult to detect objects in this phase of star formation, because they are very short-lived and they emit very little light," said Xuepeng Chen, a postdoctoral associate at Yale and lead author of the paper. The team detected the faint light emitted by the dust surrounding the object.

Most protostars are between one to 10 times as luminous as the Sun, with large dust envelopes that glow at infrared wavelengths. Because L1448-IRS2E is less than one tenth as luminous as the Sun, the team believes the object is too dim to be considered a true protostar. Yet they also discovered that the object is ejecting streams of high-velocity gas from its center, confirming that some sort of preliminary mass has already formed and the object has developed beyond the prestellar phase. This kind of outflow is seen in protostars (as a result of the magnetic field surrounding the forming star), but has not been seen at such an early stage until now.

The team hopes to use the new Herchel space telescope, launched last May, to look for more of these objects caught between the earliest stages of star formation so they can better understand how stars grow and evolve. "Stars are defined by their mass, but we still don't know at what stage of the formation process a star acquires most of its mass," said Héctor Arce, assistant professor of astronomy at Yale and an author of the paper. "This is one of the big questions driving our work."

Other authors of the paper include Qizhou Zhang and Tyler Bourke of the Harvard-Smithsonian Center for Astrophysics; and Ralf Launhardt, Markus Schmalzl and Thomas Henning of the Max Planck Institute for Astronomy.

Documentaries

I have demonstrated this technique with articles that I have prepared, using material taken from public and educational websites. The same technique can be used with material from textbooks, and other similar literature. Of course, you might want to photocopy or scan such information, before using your highlighter pens.

However, students absorb information from a variety of media. How are you going to use highlighter pens, when watching a documentary? After all, the title of this book was taken from a popular-style documentary series.

The technique that you adopt will depend on whether you are watching as a family, or whether the documentary is being used for serious study. Creation speaker Carl Kerby had some apposite things to say on this subject, in his book *Remote Control.*

One way we put this [critical thinking] into practice was while watching movies. It became a contest to see who could be the first to spot evolution, "millions of years", and other teachings that go contrary to the Word of God. After a while, we had to switch the rules around when we found ourselves starting and stopping the movie so many times. It

sometimes took forever to get through a single movie. We decided at that point to just take notes throughout the movie and discuss the movie once it was over.[1]

While it is probably not appropriate to stop the movie for every occurrence that could be addressed, we have found, in our family, that stopping the movie can often be very necessary. It is very, very rare indeed, these days, for us to watch anything as it is being broadcast. So many technologies exist today, where broadcasts can be paused for discussion - technologies such as internet streaming, and digital video recorders, as well as DVDs and Blue Rays. The techniques that Carl used have certainly influenced the next generation. His son, Carl Jnr, has applied similar techniques in his book about video games.[2]

If you don't want to take family notes, you at least need to make sure that your family knows these three categories of unscientific terms - fuzzy words, magic words and words of worldview bias. It is these ideas that you need to be able to spot. Try stopping a movie, when an evolutionary idea comes up, and discuss what category it fits into.

[1] Kerby, C. (2006), *Remote Control,* (Green Forest, AR: Master Books), p12

[2] Kerby Jnr, C and Thorwall, D (2013), *It's Not Just a Game,* (Apolomedia)

If you are using the video for study, however, you will need something more rigorous. Try dividing a notepad into 3 columns. Then each wide column can have a narrow column to the right. Give the three big columns headings - Fuzzy Words, Magic Words, and Worldview Bias. Every time you need to make a note, pause the video, jot down what has been said, or seen, under the appropriate heading, then add the time code in the narrow column. That way, you will be able to find the same information again when you need it.

None of this should spoil your enjoyment of a movie. But it is important that Christians be informed about what they are subconsciously learning, and especially what their young people are uncritically absorbing. That is why the practical aspect of this book is so important, and I hope you will read and re-read this chapter, until its concepts become automatic, when faced with any sort of education or information.

Notes

Chapter 7

FINAL CONCLUSIONS

The overriding aim of this book has been to restore confidence in Christians. One of the most common reasons for people giving up biblical truth has been their inability to know how to defend it. So, clever sounding phrases have bamboozled us into thinking that the "clever" people know best, so we had better capitulate.

I realized very early on in my Christian walk that evolution was about smoke and mirrors. It is about conjecture and imagination, and not about actual science. As I have repeatedly said, the evidence for evolution, in a museum, is not found behind the glass of the case. Rather it is in the use of language on the label. This language can be challenged, and a degree in science is not required to challenge it. Your qualifications for challenging evolution are your ability to speak, hear, write and read English.

Practice Highlighting

In order to get used to spotting these three types of evolutionary language, I suggest using the worksheets included in

this book. There will also be a workbook available soon, in which you will be able to write notes and answers.

I am always collecting these worksheets, so I will publish further sheets in pdf form on this book's website - www.justsixdays.com/wbeh

Textbooks

I am not recommending that you use highlighters in textbooks! Unless, of course, you own the textbook. Even then, I would suggest that copies be made, before highlighting.

Television Documentaries

It will do no good drawing on the TV screen with a highlighter! However, the principle remains the same.

If you are working on a documentary by yourself, I would suggest having a notebook and pencil, to remind yourself of places where the narrative fits with fuzzy words, magic words or worldview bias. Alternatively, if you are watching the documentary as a family, then it might be a good idea to watch a non-"live" version -

e.g. a DVD, downloaded mp4, or network streamed version. Then, when a notable issue comes up, you can hit the pause button and discuss the point made.

Pass It On

I believe this technique is so important, that I want to see it used more widely, and passed on. So try to use these techniques in different forums.

1. Use the materials in Sunday School. And don't just lecture! Get some copies of the materials, and highlighter pens, and get them highlighting texts!

2. Use in small groups. In a small group, you can more easily work together as a team.

3. Use in Christian Schools, or homeschool situations. Children need to know how critically to think through these issues.

4. Use in the family. Train your own children in the way they should go, encouraging them to criticize the documents, texts and documentaries from which they are learning.

5. Use social media. Please flag up these ideas across Twitter, Facebook and other places. It is my intention to hold online training seminars, using Google Hangouts.

Pray and Study

The Apostle Paul said this to Timothy:

> *Do your best to present yourself to God as one approved, a worker who has no need to be ashamed, rightly handling the word of truth. (2 Timothy 2:15 ESV)*

The old KJV says to "study to show yourself approved...". Presenting oneself to God requires us to study His word, and not to be sidetracked. Isn't it good to know, now, that the pseudo-scientific propaganda against God now no longer needs to be addressed in great detail, because it is shown to fail, when presented before the world, as a viable system.

I have presented a system, or scheme, to help you undercut the propaganda that is launched against Christians. By itself, therefore, this technique could be dry and negative. The positive aspect to "presenting yourself approved" is correctly to study "the word of truth". This book is not a substitute for getting your apologetics from the Bible. It is, at best, just a confidence builder, to reassure you that what you have learned from God's word is the truth; the ultimate truth.

Appendix

FURTHER WORKSHEETS

This appendix contains several more examples of worksheets for Fuzzy Word Analysis. All articles are taken from standard science educational websites and news agencies, and are included here under "fair use".

I would suggest that you copy the page or pages before highlighting them, using the techniques described above. Further science articles will be made available for you to use for further FWA. These will be available as pdf files at the landing page for this book - www.justsixdays.com/wbeh

The following worksheets have been made available.

- Scientists decode DNA of 'Living Fossil' Fish

- With Mix of Human and Ape-like Traits, ancient creature is puzzle for evolutionary family tree

- New model of cosmic stickiness favors 'Big Rip' demise of universe

- Dark Matter Experiment Has Detected Nothing, Researchers Say Proudly

- How the Genetic Blueprints for Limbs Came from Fish

- Humans emerged from male pig and female chimp, world's top geneticist says

- Life DID begin on Mars - then we all travelled to Earth on a meteorite

- Shrinking dinosaurs evolved into flying birds

Sample Science Article

Scientists Decode DNA of `Living Fossil' Fish

Example of an African coelacanth (Latimeria chalumnae).

Scientists have decoded the DNA of a celebrated "living
fossil" fish, gaining new insights into how today's
mammals, amphibians, reptiles and birds evolved from a
fish ancestor.

The African coelacanth (SEE-lah-kanth) is closely related to the fish lineage that started to move toward a major
evolutionary transformation, living on land And it hasn't
changed much from its ancestors of even 300 million years ago, researchers said.

At one time, scientists thought coelacanths died out some 70   million years ago. But in a startling discovery in 1938, a South African fish trawler caught a living specimen. Its close resemblance to its ancient ancestors earned it the "living fossil" nickname.

And in line with that, analysis shows its genes have been
remarkably slow to change, an international team of
researchers reported Wednesday in the journal Nature.

Maybe that's because the sea caves where the coelacanth lives provide such a stable

environment, said Kerstin Lindblad-Toh, senior author of the paper and a gene expert at the Broad Institute in Cambridge, Mass.

Modern coelacanths make up two endangered species that live off the east coast of Africa and off Indonesia. They grow to more than 5 feet long and have fleshy fins.

The coelacanth's DNA code, called its genome, is slightly smaller than a human's. Using it as a starting point, the researchers found evidence of changes in genes and in gene-controlling "switches" that evidently aided the move onto land. They involve such things as sense of smell, the immune system and limb development.

Further study of the genome may give more insights into the transition to living on land, they said. Their analysis concluded that a different creature, the lungfish, is the closest living fish relative of animals with limbs, like mammals, but they said the lungfish genome is too big to decode.

The water-to-land transition took tens of millions of years, with limbs developing in primarily aquatic animals as long as nearly 400 million years ago, by some accounts, and a true switchover to life on land by maybe 340 million years ago, said researcher Ted Daeschler, curator of vertebrate zoology at the Academy of Natural Sciences of Drexel University in Philadelphia, who didn't participate in the new work, said genome research provides a way to tackle some previously unanswerable questions in evolution.

He emphasized that DNA is best used in combination with fossils.

"This is a great detective tool," he said. "You might collect DNA evidence at a crime scene, but you can't ignore the dead body.... With paleontology, we have the dead bodies."

Information taken from the NewsMax and Associated Press,

Sample Science Article

With mix of human and apelike traits, ancient creature is puzzle for evolutionary family tree

Published April 11, 2013, Associated Press

http://www.foxnews.com/science/2013/04/11/with-mix-human-and-apelike-traits-ancient-creature-is-puzzle-for-evolutionary/

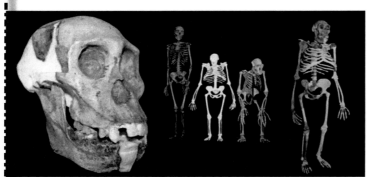

This undated image provided by Lee R. Berger and the University of the Witwatersrand shows a reconstructed skull and jaw of Australopithecus sediba. The newly-studied species lived some 2 million years ago, and it both climbed in trees and walked upright. Scientists are getting a more comprehensive look at the extinct South African creature with an intriguing mix of human-like and primitive traits, but scientists say they still haven't pinned down where it fits on our evolutionary family tree.

Scientists have gained new insights into an extinct South African creature with an intriguing mix of human and apelike traits, and apparently an unusual way of walking. But they still haven't pinned down where it fits on our evolutionary family tree.

It will take more fossil discoveries to sort that out.

The human branch of the evolutionary tree, called Homo, is thought to have arisen from a group of ancient species called australopithecines. The newly studied species is a member of this group, and so its similarities to humans are enticing for tackling the riddle of how Homo appeared.

It's called Australopithecus sediba (aw-STRAL-oh-PITH-uh-kus se-DEE-bah), which means "southern ape, wellspring." It lived some 2 million years ago, and it both climbed in trees and walked upright. Its remains were discovered in 2008 when the 9-year-old son of a paleoanthropologist accidently came across a bone in South Africa.

A 2011 analysis of some of A. sediba's bones showed a combination of human and more apelike traits, like a snapshot of evolution in action. That theme continues in six papers published online Thursday by the journal Science, which complete the initial examination of two partial skeletons and an isolated shinbone.

Jeremy DeSilva of Boston University, lead author of one of the papers, said the fossils reveal an unexpected "mosaic of anatomies."

"I didn't think you could have this combination, that hand with that pelvis with that foot... And yet, there it is," he said.

DeSilva said he has no idea how A. sediba is related to humans, noting that the different traits argue for different conclusions.

Among the new analyses, the ribs show the creature's upper trunk resembled an ape's, while the lower part looked more like a human's. Arm bones other than the hand and wrist look primitive, reflecting climbing ability, while earlier analysis of the hand had shown mixed traits.

The teeth also show a mix of human and primitive features, and provide new evidence that A. sediba is closely related to early humans, said Debbie Guatelli-Steinberg of Ohio State University, a co-author of a dental analysis. It and an older South African species, A. africanus, appear more closely related to early humans than other australopithecines like the famous "Lucy" are, she said.

But she said the analysis can't determine which of the two species is the closer relative, nor whether A. sediba is a direct ancestor of humans.

Another study found a mix of human and apelike traits in leg bones, and concluded that A. sediba walked like no other known animal.

Its heel was narrow like an ape's, which would seem to prevent walking upright, but the more humanlike knee, pelvis and hip show A. sediba did just that, DeSilva said.

When people walk, they strike the ground with the heel first. But that would be disastrous from A. sediba's narrow heel bone, so instead the creature struck the ground first with the outside of the foot, DeSilva and co-authors propose. The foot would react by rolling inward, which is called pronation. In people, chronic pronation can cause pain in the foot, knees, hip and back, said DeSilva, who tried out the ancient creature's gait.

"I've been walking around campus this way, and it hurts," he said.

But the bones of A. sediba show features that evidently prevented those pain problems, he said. The creature apparently adopted this gait as a kind of compromise for a body that had to climb trees proficiently as well as walk upright, he said.

Information taken from the Fox News, and used under 'fair use' for educational purposes.

Sample Science Article
New model of cosmic stickiness favors 'Big Rip' demise of universe

PUBLISHED: June 30, 2015, AUTHOR: David Salisbury

Read more:
http://www.sciencedaily.com/releases/2015/06/150630155221.htm

The universe can be a very sticky place, but just how sticky is a matter of debate.

That is because for decades cosmologists have had trouble reconciling the classic notion of viscosity based on the laws of thermodynamics with Einstein's general theory of relativity. However, a team from Vanderbilt University has come up with a fundamentally new mathematical formulation of the problem that appears to bridge this long-standing gap.

The new math has some significant implications for the ultimate fate of the universe. It tends to favor one of the more radical scenarios that cosmologists have come up with known as the "Big Rip." It may also shed new light on the basic nature of dark energy.

This is a time line of life of the universe that ends in a Big Rip.

Credit: Jeremy Teaford, Vanderbilt University

The new approach was developed by Assistant Professor of Mathematics Marcelo Disconzi in collaboration with physics professors Thomas Kephart and Robert Scherrer and is described in a paper published earlier this year in the journal Physical Review D.

"Marcelo has come up with a simpler and more elegant formulation that is mathematically sound and obeys all the applicable physical laws," said Scherrer.

The type of viscosity that has cosmological relevance is different from the familiar "ketchup" form of viscosity, which is called shear viscosity and is a measure of a fluid's resistance to flowing through small openings like the neck of a ketchup bottle. Instead, cosmological viscosity is a form of bulk viscosity, which is the measure of a fluid's resistance to expansion or contraction. The reason we don't often deal with bulk viscosity in everyday life is because most liquids we encounter cannot be compressed or expanded very much.

Disconzi began by tackling the problem of relativistic fluids. Astronomical objects that produce this phenomenon include supernovae (exploding stars) and neutron stars (stars that have been crushed down to the size of planets).

Scientists have had considerable success modeling what happens when ideal fluids -- those with no viscosity -- are boosted to near-light speeds. But almost all fluids are viscous in nature and, despite decades of effort, no one

Sample Science Article

has managed to come up with a generally accepted way to handle viscous fluids traveling at relativistic velocities. In the past, the models formulated to predict what happens when these more realistic fluids are accelerated to a fraction of the speed of light have been plagued with inconsistencies: the most glaring of which has been predicting certain conditions where these fluids could travel faster than the speed of light.

"This is disastrously wrong," said Disconzi, "since it is well-proven experimentally that nothing can travel faster than the speed of light."

These problems inspired the mathematician to re-formulate the equations of relativistic fluid dynamics in a way that does not exhibit the flaw of allowing faster-than-light speeds. He based his approach on one that was advanced in the 1950s by French mathematician André Lichnerowicz.

Next, Disconzi teamed up with Kephart and Scherrer to apply his equations to broader cosmological theory. This produced a number of interesting results, including some potential new insights into the mysterious nature of dark energy.

In the 1990s, the physics community was shocked when astronomical measurements showed that the universe is expanding at an ever-accelerating rate. To explain this unpredicted acceleration, they were forced to hypothesize the existence of an unknown form of repulsive energy that is spread throughout the universe. Because they knew so little about it, they labeled it "dark energy."

Most dark energy theories to date have not taken cosmic viscosity into account, despite the fact that it has a repulsive effect strikingly similar to that of dark energy. "It is possible, but not very likely, that viscosity could account for all the acceleration that has been attributed to dark energy," said Disconzi. "It is more likely that a significant fraction of the acceleration could be due to this more prosaic cause. As a result, viscosity may act as an important constraint on the properties of dark energy."

Another interesting result involves the ultimate fate of the universe. Since the discovery of the universe's runaway expansion, cosmologists have come up with a number of dramatic scenarios of what it could mean for the future.

One scenario, dubbed the "Big Freeze," predicts that after 100 trillion years or so the universe will have grown so vast that the supplies of gas will become too thin for stars to form. As a result, existing stars will gradually burn out, leaving only black holes which, in turn, slowly evaporate away as space itself gets colder and colder.

An even more radical scenario is the "Big Rip." It is predicated on a type of "phantom" dark energy that gets stronger over time. In this case, the expansion rate of the universe becomes so great that in 22 billion years or so material objects begin to fall apart and individual atoms disassemble themselves into unbound elementary particles and radiation.

The key value involved in this scenario is the ratio between dark energy's pressure and density, what is called its equation of state parameter. If this value drops below -1 then the universe will eventually be pulled apart. Cosmologists have called this the "phantom barrier." In previous models with viscosity the universe could not evolve beyond this limit.

In the Desconzi-Kephart-Scherrer formulation, however, this barrier does not exist. Instead, it provides a natural way for the equation of state parameter to fall below -1.

"In previous models with viscosity the Big Rip was not possible," said Scherrer. "In this new model, viscosity actually drives the universe toward this extreme end state."

According to the scientists, the results of their pen-and-paper analyses of this new formulation for relativistic viscosity are quite promising but a much deeper analysis must be carried out to determine its viability. The only way to do this is to use powerful computers to analyze the complex equations numerically. In this fashion the scientists can make predictions that can be compared with experiment and observation.

Sample Science Article

Dark Matter Experiment Has Detected Nothing, Researchers Say Proudly

By Dennis Overbye, PUBLISHED: October 30th 2013

Read more: http://www.nytimes.com/2013/10/31/science/space/dark-matter-experiment-has-found-nothing-scientists-say-

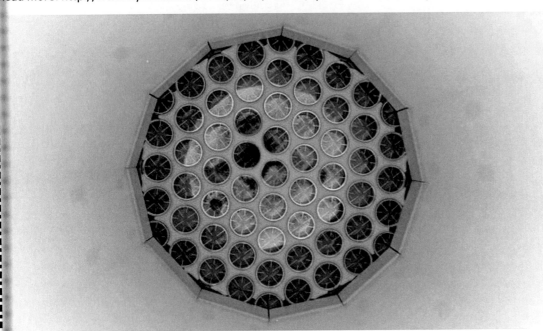

Inside the Large Underground Xenon dark matter detector. (Photo: Matthew Kapust/South Dakota Science and Technology Authority)

The former Homestake Gold Mine in Lead, S.D., has a hallowed place in the history of physics as a spot where nothing happens.

It was there, in the 1970s, that Raymond Davis Jr. attempted to catch neutrinos, spooky subatomic particles emitted by the sun, in a vat of cleaning fluid a mile underground and for a long time came up empty. For revolutionizing the study of those particles, he shared the Nobel Prize in Physics in 2002.

On Wednesday, an international team of physicists based in the same cavern of the former mine announced a new milestone of frustration, but also hope — this time in the search for dark matter, the mysterious, invisible ingredient that astronomers say makes up a quarter of the cosmos.

In the first three months of running the biggest, most sensitive dark matter detector yet — a vat of 368 kilograms of liquid xenon cooled to minus 150 degrees Fahrenheit — the researchers said they had not seen a trace of the clouds of particles that theorists say should be wafting through space, the galaxy, the Earth and, of course, ourselves, knocking out at least one controversial class of dark matter candidates.

But the experiment has just begun and will run for all of next year. The detector already twice as sensitive as the next best one, will gain another factor of sensitivity in the coming run.

"Just because we don't see anything in the first run doesn't mean we won't see anything in the second," said Richard Gaitskell, a professor of physics at Brown University and a spokesman for an international collaboration that operates the experiment known as LUX, for the Large Underground Xenon dark matter experiment.

As has become de rigueur for such occasions, the scientists took pride and hope in how clearly they did not see anything. "In 25 years of searching, this is the cleanest signal I've ever seen," Dr. Gaitskell said in an interview.

That meant, the scientists said, that their detector was working so well that they would easily see a dark matter particle if and when it decided to drop by.

Sample Science Article

In this case, they had support from outside scientists. Neal Weiner, a particle theorist at New York University, called the results impressive.

"They have not found dark matter," he said. "There is nothing smacking you in the face to make you think there is something there." But as the sensitivity of the detector increases, he added, "If there is anything in there, it should become apparent."

The announcement at the Homestake site capped a morning of ceremony, which included Gov. Dennis Daugaard of South Dakota and members of the State Legislature, at what amounted to a coming-out party for LUX and for the Sanford Underground Research Facility, a lab being developed in the old mine with a mix of state and private money, as well as support from the Energy Department. The lab is named after the philanthropist T. Denny Sanford, who donated $70 million to get it going.

LUX is the latest in a long series of ever-larger experiments that have occupied and taunted the world's physicists over the last few years. They are all in abandoned mines or other underground places to shield them from cosmic rays, which could cause false alarms. Daniel McKinsey, an associate professor of physics at Yale and a spokesman for the LUX group, said in an interview that the biggest source of noise in the LUX device was trace radioactivity in the detector itself.

Larger instruments are already on the drawing boards of LUX and other collaborations, but physicists say the experiments are already sensitive enough to test some versions of dark matter that have been proposed, including the idea that dark particles interact with ordinary matter by exchanging the recently discovered Higgs boson. Dr. Weiner said he held his breath every time new results from a dark matter experiment were released.

Dark matter has teased and tantalized physicists since the 1970s, when it was demonstrated that some invisible material must be providing the gravitational glue to hold galaxies together. Determining what it is would provide insight into particles and forces not described by the Standard Model that now rules physics, not to mention a slew of Nobel Prizes.

Physicists' best guess is that this dark matter consists of clouds of exotic subatomic particles left over from the Big Bang and known generically as WIMPs, for weakly interacting massive particles, which would weigh several hundred times as much as a proton but could nevertheless pass through the Earth like smoke through a screen door. They are a generic feature of a much-hyped idea known as supersymmetry.

Particle physicists have been hoping to produce these particles or other evidence of supersymmetry in the Large Hadron Collider outside Geneva or to read their signature in cosmic rays from outer space. No one has ever claimed to have seen such a heavy WIMP, in space or underground, but another experiment in another mine, the Cryogenic Dark Matter Search, claims to have recorded three events that could have been low-mass dark matter particles, only a few times heavier than a proton.

The new results from the Homestake mine, if they are correct, would rule out those low-mass particles. Dr. Gaitskell explained that if those particles were real, the Homestake detector would have recorded 1,550 of them.

"If there are 1,550 of them, boy are we going to see them," he said in a presentation at the Homestake facility on Wednesday. "We do not see the low-mass WIMPS."

But afterward, Juan I. Collar, a dark matter specialist at the University of Chicago who has been urging the community to take low-mass WIMPs seriously, questioned whether the LUX detector had been adequately calibrated to detect them.

"They do have a real interest in performing those calibrations, because they would settle the issue," Dr. Collar said in an email. "We just have to be patient. At the end they promised to do so, and I have no doubts they will."

For now, a quarter of the universe is still missing in action.

Sample Science Article

How the Genetic Blueprints for Limbs Came from Fish

PUBLISHED: January 21st 2014 Read more: http://www.sciencedaily.com/releases/2014/01/140121183412.htm

The transition from water to land is one of the most fascinating enigmas of evolution. In particular, the evolution of limbs from ancestral fish fins remains a mystery. Both fish and land animals possess clusters of Hoxa and Hoxd genes, which are necessary for both fin and limb formation during embryonic development.

Denis Duboule's team, at the UNIGE and the EPFL, Switzerland, compared the structure and behavior of these gene clusters in embryos from mice and zebrafish. The researchers discovered similar 3-dimensional DNA organization of the fish and mouse clusters, which indicates that the main mechanism used to pattern tetrapod limbs was already present in fish. However, when inserted into transgenic mouse embryos, the fish Hox genes were only active in the mouse arm but not in the digits, showing that the fish DNA lacks essential genetic elements for digit formation. The study, published in the January 21, 2014 edition of PLoS Biology, thus concludes that, although the digital part of the limbs evolved as a novelty in land animals, this happened by elaborating on an ancestral, pre-existing DNA infrastructure.

Our first four-legged land ancestor came out of the sea some 350 million years ago. Watching a lungfish, our closest living fish relative, crawl on its four pointed fins gives us an idea of what the first evolutionary steps on land probably looked like. However, the transitional path between fin structural elements in fish and limbs in tetrapods remains elusive.

An ancestral regulatory strategy …
In animals, the Hox genes, often referred to as 'architect genes', are responsible for organizing the body structures during embryonic

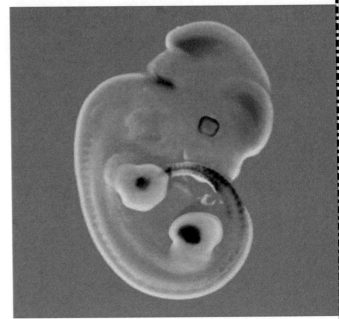

This shows the expression of fish Hox genes in a mouse embryo. (Credit: Denis Duboule, UNIGE)

development. Both fish and mammals possess clusters of Hoxa and Hoxd genes, which are necessary for fin and limb formation. The team of Denis Duboule, professor at the University of Geneva (UNIGE) and the Ecole polytechnique fédérale de Lausanne (EPFL), Switzerland, had recently shown that, during mammalian development, Hoxd genes depend on a 'bimodal' 3-dimensional DNA structure to direct the development of the characteristic subdivision of the limbs into arm and paw, a division which is absent from fish fins.

'To determine where the genetics behind this subdivision into 'hand' and 'arm' came from during evolution, we decided to closely compare the genetic processes at work in both fin and limb development', says Joost Woltering, researcher at the Department of Genetics and

Sample Science Article

Evolution of the UNIGE Faculty of Science and lead author of the study. Surprisingly, the researchers found a similar bimodal 3-dimensional chromatin architecture in the Hoxd gene region in zebrafish embryos. These findings indicate that the regulatory mechanism used to pattern tetrapod limbs probably predates the divergence between fish and tetrapods. "In fact this finding was a great surprise as we expected that this 'bimodal' DNA conformation was exactly what would make all the difference in the genetics for making limbs or making fins" adds Joost Woltering.

…that just needs to be modernized

Does this imply that digits are homologous to distal fin structures in fish? To answer this question, the geneticists inserted into mice embryos the genomic regions that regulate Hox gene expression in fish fins. 'As another surprise, regulatory regions from fish triggered

Hox gene expression predominantly in the arm and not in the digits. Altogether, this suggests that our digits evolved during the fin to limb transition by modernizing an already existing regulatory mechanism', explains Denis Duboule.

'A good metaphor for what has probably happened would be the process of 'retrofitting', as is done in engineering to equip outdated machine frames with new technology. Only, in this case, it was a primitive DNA architecture which evolved new 'technology' to make the fingers and toes', says Joost Woltering.

Fin radials are not homologous to tetrapod digits

The researchers conclude that, although fish possess the Hox regulatory toolkit to produce digits, this potential is not utilized as it is in tetrapods. Therefore, they propose that fin radials, the bony elements of fins, are not homologous to tetrapod digits, although they rely in part on a shared regulatory strategy.

New lines of investigation are to find out exactly what has changed between the DNA elements in fish and tetrapods. 'By now we know a lot of genetic switches in mice that drive Hox expression in the digits. It is key to find out exactly how these processes work nowadays to understand what made digits appear and favor the colonization of the terrestrial environment', concludes Denis Duboule.

Journal Reference

Joost M. Woltering, Daan Noordermeer, Marion Leleu, Denis Duboule. Conservation and Divergence of Regulatory Strategies at Hox Loci and the Origin of Tetrapod Digits. PLoS Biology, 2014; 12 (1): e1001773 DOI: 10.1371/journal.pbio.1001773

This material is taken from Université de Genève (2014, January 21). How the genetic blueprints for limbs came from fish. ScienceDaily. Retrieved January 23, 2014, from http://www.sciencedaily.com /releases/2014/01/140121183412.htm

Sample Science Article

Humans emerged from male pig and female chimp, world's top

By Kounteya Sinha, TNN Nov 30, 2013

Read more: http://articles.timesofindia.indiatimes.com/2013-11-30/science/44595591_1_humans-chimpanzees-traits

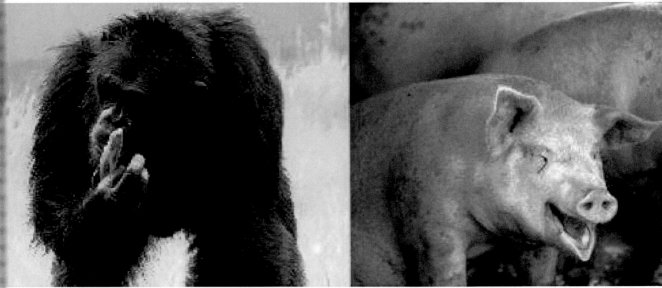

University of Georgia's Dr Eugene McCarthy has suggested that humans didn't evolve from just apes but was a backcross hybrid of a chimpanzee and pigs.

LONDON: Humans are actually hybrids, who emerged as an offspring of a male pig and a female chimpanzee, according to one of the world's leading geneticist.

Turning the theory of human ancestry on its head, Dr Eugene McCarthy — one of the world's leading authorities on hybridization in animals from the University of Georgia has suggested that humans didn't evolve from just apes but was a backcross hybrid of a chimpanzee and pigs.

His hypothesis is based on the fact that though humans have many features in common with chimps, there are a lot more that don't correspond to any other primates. He then suggests that there is only one animal in the animal kingdom that has all of the traits which distinguish humans from our primate cousins.

"What is this other animal that has all these traits? The answer is Sus scrofa - the ordinary pig" he says.

He explains: "Genetically, we're close to chimpanzees, and yet we have many physical traits that distinguish us from chimpanzees. One fact, however, suggests the need for an open mind: as it turns out, many features that distinguish humans from chimpanzees also distinguish them from all other primates. Features found in human beings, but not in other primates, cannot be accounted for by hybridization of a primate with some other primate. If hybridization is to explain such features, the cross will have to be between a chimpanzee and

Sample Science Article

a non-primate - an unusual, distant cross to create an unusual creature."

Dr McCarthy suggests that Charles Darwin told only half the story of human evolution.

"We believe that humans are related to chimpanzees because humans share so many traits with chimpanzees. Is it not rational then also, if pigs have all the traits that distinguish humans from other primates, to suppose that humans are also related to pigs? Let us take it as our hypothesis, then, that humans are the product of ancient hybridization between pig and chimpanzee," he said.

According to Dr McCarthy, if we compare humans with non-mammals or invertebrates like the crocodile, bullfrog, octopus, dragonfly and starfish, pigs and chimpanzees suddenly seem quite similar to humans.

Pigs and chimpanzees differ in chromosome counts. The opinion is often expressed that when two animals differ in this way, they cannot produce fertile hybrids. This rule is, however, only a generalization. While such differences do tend to have an adverse effect on the fertility of hybrid offspring, it is also true that many different types of crosses in which the parents differ in chromosome counts produce hybrids that capable themselves of producing offspring.

There is substantial evidence supporting the idea that very distantly related mammals can mate and produce a hybrid.

Another suggestive fact, Dr McCarthy says is the frequent use of pigs in the surgical treatment of human beings. Pig heart valves are used to replace those of human coronary patients. Pig skin is used in the treatment of human burn victims. "Serious

efforts are now underway to transplant kidneys and other organs from pigs into human beings. Why are pigs suited for such purposes? Why not goats, dogs, or bears - animals that, in terms of taxonomic classification, are no more distantly related to human beings than pigs?," he said.

"It might seem unlikely that a pig and a chimpanzee would choose to mate, but their behaviour patterns and reproductive anatomy does, in fact, make them compatible. It is, of course, a well-established fact that animals sometimes attempt to mate with individuals that are unlike themselves, even in a natural setting, and that many of these crosses successfully produce hybrid offspring," he adds.

Dr Eugene McCarthy says that the fact that even modern-day humans are relatively infertile may be significant in this connection.

"If a hybrid population does not die out altogether, it will tend to improve in fertility with each passing generation under the pressure of natural selection. Fossils indicate that we have had at least 200,000 years to recover our fertility since the time that the first modern humans (Homo sapiens) appeared. The earliest creatures generally recognized as human ancestors (Ardipithecus, Orrorin) date to about six million years ago. So our fertility has had a very long time to improve. If we have been recovering for thousands of generations and still show obvious symptoms of sterility, then our earliest human ancestors, if they were hybrids, must have suffered from an infertility that was quite severe. This line of reasoning, too, suggests that the chimpanzee might have produced Homo sapiens by crossing with a genetically incompatible mate, possibly even one outside the primate order," he said.

Sample Science Article

Life DID begin on Mars - then we all travelled to Earth on a meteorite

Element crucial to the origin of life 'would only have been available on the red planet'

By ELLIE ZOLFAGHARIFARD

PUBLISHED: 17:07 EST, 28 August 2013 | UPDATED: 17:07 EST, 28 August 2013

Read more: http://www.dailymail.co.uk/sciencetech/article-2404416/Life-DID-begin-Mars--travelled-Earth-meteorite-Element-crucial-origin-life-available-red-planet.html#ixzz2dqAZOnyg

- **Molybdenum mineral is thought to have been crucial to the origin of life**

- **Material may have been available on the surface of Mars and not on Earth**

- **This could suggest that life came to Earth on a Martian meteorite**

It might not just be men who are from Mars, claims a new study which suggests that all life on Earth actually began on the red planet.

An element believed to be crucial to the origin of life would only have been available on the surface of Mars, it is claimed.

Geochemist Professor Steven Benner argues that the 'seeds' of life probably arrived on Earth in meteorites blasted off Mars by impacts or volcanic eruptions.

As evidence he points to the oxidised mineral form of the element molybdenum, thought to be a catalyst that helped organic molecules develop into the first living structures.

Professor Benner will present his findings to geochemists gathering today at the annual Goldschmidt conference.

'In addition recent studies show that these conditions, suitable for the origin of life, may still exist on Mars,' said Professor Benner, of the Westheimer Institute for Science and Technology in Gainesville, Florida.

'It's only when molybdenum becomes highly oxidised that it is able to influence how early life formed.

'This form of molybdenum couldn't have been available on Earth at the time life first began, because

Professor Steven Benner will tell geochemists gathering today at the annual Goldschmidt conference that an oxidised mineral form of the element molybdenum, which may have been crucial to the origin of life, could only have been available on the surface of Mars and not on Earth

three billion years ago the surface of the Earth had very little oxygen, but Mars did.

'It's yet another piece of evidence which makes it more likely life came to Earth on a Martian meteorite, rather than starting on this planet.'

Sample Science Article

Molybdenum can be mined from becomes Molybdenite (pictured). Scientists believe the oxidised form of molybdenum was available on

The research Professor Benner will present at the conference tackles two of the paradoxes which make it difficult for scientists to understand how life could have started on Earth.

The first is dubbed by Professor Benner as the 'tar paradox'.

All living things are made of organic matter, but if you add energy such as heat or light to organic molecules and leave them to themselves, they don't create life.

Instead, they turn into something more like tar, oil or asphalt.

Prof Benner added: 'Certain elements seem able to control the propensity of organic materials to turn into tar, particularly boron and molybdenum, so we believe that minerals containing both were fundamental to life first starting.

'Analysis of a Martian meteorite recently showed that there was boron on Mars; we now believe that the oxidised form of molybdenum was there too.'

The second paradox is that life would have struggled to start on the early Earth because it was likely to have been totally covered by water.

Not only would this have prevented sufficient concentrations of boron forming - it's currently only found in very dry places such as Death Valley - but water is corrosive to RNA, which scientists believe was the first genetic molecule to appear.

Although there was water on Mars, it covered much smaller areas than on early Earth.

Prof Benner said: 'The evidence seems to be building that we are actually all Martians; that life started on Mars and came to Earth on a rock.

'It's lucky that we ended up here nevertheless, as certainly Earth has been the better of the two planets for sustaining life.

'If our hypothetical Martian ancestors had remained on Mars, there might not have been a story to tell.'

Analysis of a Martian meteorite recently showed that there was boron on Mars (pictured). Boron is thought to be another key element for life

Shrinking dinosaurs evolved into flying birds

Science Daily, 7/31/2013

Read more: http://www.sciencedaily.com/releases/2014/07/140731145559.htm

A new study involving scientists from the University of Southampton has revealed how massive, meat-eating, ground-dwelling dinosaurs evolved into agile flying birds: they just kept shrinking and shrinking, for over 50 million years.

Meet the ancestors: The feathered dinosaur Microraptor pounces on a nest of primitive birds (Sinornis). Both species lived during the Cretaceous Period (~120 million years ago) in what is now northern China.

Today, in the journal Science, the researchers present a detailed family tree of dinosaurs and their bird descendants, which maps out this unlikely transformation.

They showed that the branch of theropod dinosaurs, which gave rise to modern birds, were the only dinosaurs that kept getting inexorably smaller.

"These bird ancestors also evolved new adaptations, such as feathers, wishbones and wings, four times faster than other dinosaurs," says co-author Darren Naish, Vertebrate Palaeontologist at the University of Southampton.

"Birds evolved through a unique phase of sustained miniaturisation in dinosaurs," says lead author Associate Professor Michael Lee, from the University of Adelaide's School of Earth and Environmental Sciences and the South Australian Museum.

"Being smaller and lighter in the land of giants, with rapidly evolving anatomical adaptations, provided these bird ancestors with new ecological opportunities, such as the ability to climb trees, glide and fly. Ultimately, this evolutionary flexibility helped birds survive the deadly meteorite impact which killed off all their dinosaurian cousins."

Co-author Gareth Dyke, Senior Lecturer in Vertebrate Palaeontology at the University of Southampton, adds: "The dinosaurs most closely related to birds are all small, and many of them -- such as the aptly named Microraptor -- had some ability to climb and glide."

The study examined over 1,500 anatomical traits of dinosaurs to reconstruct their family tree. The researchers used sophisticated mathematical modelling to trace evolving adaptions and changing body size over time and across dinosaur branches.

The international team also included Andrea Cau, from the University of Bologna and Museo Geologico Giovanni Capellini.

The study concluded that the branch of dinosaurs leading to birds was more evolutionary innovative than other dinosaur lineages. "Birds out-shrank and out-evolved their dinosaurian ancestors, surviving where their larger, less evolvable relatives could not," says Associate Professor Lee.

Made in the USA
San Bernardino, CA
20 October 2015